THE BIG MEETING

A people's view of the Durham Miners' Gala

Edited by Keith Armstrong
Associate Editor: Andy Croft

Published by Trade Union Printing Services in association with 'Northern Voices' and Index Books

Cover photographs: Stan Gamester

'Northern Voices' is a member of the Federation of Worker Writers & Community Publishers

ISBN 1-871518-10-5

TUPS, 30 Lime Street, Newcastle upon Tyne NE1 2PG Tel. (091) 233 0990 Fax (091) 233 0578

DEDICATION

This book is dedicated to the miners of the Durham coalfield, past and present, who, with their families, suffered the hardships of a brutal industry.

We are confident that the values and principles they developed in their long struggle will survive the callous destruction of a once great industry.

CONTENTS

EDITOR'S NOTE

This book makes no claims to be a definitive history of the Big Meeting. It is a people's history, told in their own words, their poems, songs and stories.

I hope it creates a vivid impression of the cultural significance of this wonderful event and gives us hope for the future in the lessons we learn from it.

The book has been long in the making and I thank everyone who has contributed for their patience. I hope the wait has been worthwhile. Who knows, it might even stimulate a second volume of Gala stories and photographs! There is certainly more where this came from.

Keith Armstrong

KEITH ARMSTRONG is a freelance poet, qualified librarian and community publisher. He is co-ordinator of the 'Northern Voices' project which has published many booklets in which local working-class people have their say and which reflect the rich culture of North East England.

He has formed several writers' groups in the North East and was a founder-member of the 'Strong Words' publishing project.

He was Community Arts Development Worker in East Durham from 1980-1986 and a Community Worker in Newcastle during the 70s.

He has read from his poetry throughout Britain and Europe, including the European Parliament in Strasbourg, in the former Soviet Union and in Iceland (during the Cod War). He is currently working on a CD with the Durham folk band 'The Whisky Priests'.

Further information about the 'Northern Voices' project can be obtained from: 1st Floor, 28 Northumberland Square, North Shields, Tyne & Wear NE30 1PW. Tel: (091) 259 1479 or (091) 252 9531.

Seaham Lodge 1921

ACKNOWLEDGMENTS

Thanks to the many people who sent in material for this book. We are sorry not all of it could be included.

Thanks especially to those people who formed the network of co-ordinators throughout the North East: Dave Ayre and Harry French (Wear Valley); Eileen Carnaffin (Local Studies Librarian) and Dave Gaston (Gateshead); Kevin Cadwallender (Easington); Bert Draycott (Sedgefield); Benny Graham (Chester-le-Street); John B. Kirtley (Sunderland); Ralph Thompson (South Tyneside).

Thanks also to Chrisy Edge for her interviews with local women; Tony Whittle and Stan Gamester for photographic work.

The whole project was established with the assistance of Durham City Arts, supported by Durham City Council, Durham County Council and Northern Arts. Thanks also to Chester-le-Street, Easington, South Tyneside and Sunderland Councils for further financial assistance.

We are grateful to the Newcastle Chronicle and Journal, Northern Echo, Beamish Museum, and local photographers Derrik Scott and Trevor Smith for permission to reproduce photographs; to Gilesgate Junior School and teacher Clare Martin for allowing us to include extracts from their publication "In Them Days"; to Rene Chaplin for permitting us to re-print the articles by her late husband Sid; and to the NUM for access to the Red Hill archives and permission to use extracts from Gala programmes.

Many of the photographs are from private collections. We have not always been able to identify them precisely, but we have provided captions wherever possible.

FOREWORD BY TONY BENN

The Big Meeting in Durham - The Miners' Gala - has a unique place in the history of the labour movement and in the struggles of pitmen, their families and communities.

It is well over thirty years since I was first invited to speak and I have seen many ups and downs, from the high point of 1964, when Labour was elected, through to the gloom of the assault on the NUM over 20 years later, which seemed to overwhelm the union.

Successive Presidents of the Union have always reported on the problems and the prospects of the industry, and successive Labour Prime Ministers and Leaders - until quite recently - have come to the Gala to be refreshed and to renew their commitment to trade unionism and to socialism.

And for the speakers - like me - the dinner beforehand was an opportunity to meet and talk with colleagues and the many foreign visitors and diplomats who came to see what it was that gave the Gala its reputation.

At those dinners, we were all usually asked to sing songs and I recall especially Jim Callaghan singing "I am the man, the very fat man who waters the workers' beer", which was greeted with wild enthusiasm.

In 1993, as has always been the custom, the miners with their bands and banners marched into Durham Cathedral for a service that somehow seemed to emphasise the links between bible teaching and the best of socialism.

For well over 100 years, broken only by war, those Galas have been a focus for the expression of solidarity and an inspiration for socialists and progressive people.

Working underground involves risks and dangers which make the miners 100 per cent dependent on each other, and this has bred a quality of character which is markedly different from the "I'm all right Jack" philosophy of the City which gambles with the wealth those very miners have created.

Fishermen and farmworkers who also have to face the dangers of nature have a similar experience but there is no group for whom loyalty and self-sacrifice are so marked as it is with the men who have brought out the coal upon which our industrial strength is built.

The Durham Coalfield was the only coalfield that balloted to continue the strike after the long and hard conflict of 1926, and throughout the 1984/85 strike that same quality was shown time and again.

But now, in pursuit of a vicious vendetta against the NUM, every pit in the area has been closed and the mining communities have been devastated and made derelict.

In recent years, as the number of collieries diminished, the number of banners diminished too. But other coalfields and other unions brought their banners to the Gala to sustain the spirit of the occasion and to

photo Stan Gamester   Tony Benn

march past the County Hotel where each year's speakers reviewed the mass of humanity that passed beneath.

I hope that that extension of the Gala will now be completed by carrying on the tradition to make it an occasion where the whole labour movement from across the country can meet and re-dedicate itself to the struggles that lie ahead.

It is right that a book about the Gala should now be written but I hope it marks not the end of an era but the beginning of a new one to see us into the next century and beyond.

INTRODUCTION BY DAVE DOUGLASS

Youth at Big Meeting 1960s

The Gala is a sensual, emotional, experience. It has to do with deep family ties, trials and shared experiences. It has to do with friendships, the type formed in the pitch black of the mine, the comradeship that in the dark you know will be there without having to look, even suppose you could see. It has to do with politics and class identity with a mission handed on to us from before; a mission which has been entrusted to us. It has to do with regionality, ethnicity, about being from HERE, something ours which has always been ours. It is about sex, about serious thought, for some too about GOD and religion or at least faith and hope. It is about our past, it is about now and what future we aspire to. It is about every year of your life since you were a child when each year the Gala meant something different, something added to the accumulating experience. In Durham pit families, among the bairns and the teenagers, though for different reasons than their folks, it was held as highly as Christmas Day. The Gala meant a total infusion of the senses in music, in voices, in laughter and tears; a heart-thumping joy as you bounced before the majesty of the lofty banner, or stepped out determinedly at its side, swelling and breathing with the whole crowd and becoming one with the surging mass of colour and music and hope that is Durham Big Meeting. Words were not developed for imparting such a sensation, if you've felt it, you will know. Something of the story begins like this: the Cathedral City of Durham was the capital of the coalfield, though it was to gown and not the coaly pitlad to which it paid its allegiance. At times, as windows were boarded up and shops closed down, some left for the day while from others we thought we felt an icy stare. It was matterless, we didn't come for them. David Bean tells us: "One August night, ninety-three years ago, the good people of Durham barred their doors and windows, locked up their spoons and their daughters, called in police reinforcements - and waited for the worst. For the miners - those rough, savage men from the rural pits, who smashed machinery, said rude things to the gentry, beat their wives, ate their children and squandered their spare time in drink, cock-fighting and gambling - were moving on the City. They were coming, it was whispered round the timid town, "to get their reets"."

I suppose over the last forty years they've

almost got used to us, and the City is ours now, at least for Durham Big Meeting Day it must be, for Cathedral and Town are woven into our banners, and our lives.

The first formally recognised 'Big Meeting' as an annual event was staged in Wharton Park in 1871. The platform was decorated with the Thornley Banner, a lodge renowned for militant action and radical thought. It was an old centre of Chartism and was the only Durham pit village to have participated in the bold attempt at a general strike in 1839. It had been the Thornley men who first went on strike in the movement of 1869 which was finally to put an end to the hated system of the bond, just two years preceding this first Gala and, doubtless, the reason for pride of place for their lodge banner. The following year, the Gala started to be held on the racecourse. By 1875, it had become so big the North Eastern Railways withdrew all the trains between Bishop Auckland, Newcastle and Lanchester to Durham, claiming that the railway could not cope with so many people on a Saturday. In consequence, Galas in the following two years were held on Mondays, which, given the colliers' tradition of laying idle many Mondays anyway, must have pleased the owners no end. In point of fact, there had been a great many 'Big Meetings' of the miners of the twin coal counties of Northumberland and Durham. From the beginning of the 1800s, massive armies of the miners would converge from the most distant villages, from coast and hills, walking all day in many cases to reach the swaying throngs clustered round the speakers, carriers of the gospel which spelt freedom

Chopwell Banner 1950s

and an end to the tyranny of coal baron, explosion and inundation. Because of the vast distances involved, banners and lodges would be arriving from all directions and at all hours throughout the day. True to the last, the Durham Big Meeting kept this informality, without strict arrival times or even designated routes, banners converging on the County Hotel from never less than three directions. Likewise, at the end of the speakers' session, bands strike up and lodges march off again quite at will, and without central organisation.

A further feature of the mass rallies at the turn of the previous century was the practice of running two and at times three platforms concurrently; the crowds being so great, even the great public speakers of the recent past couldn't hope to reach the most distant ears. This mass of colour, diversity and decentralism adds to the popular feature that this truly is a meeting, though one coupled with carnival and fiesta.

One of the early venues of the 1830s was the Black Fell, near Eighton Banks in County Durham, where "an immense number of pitmen from the collieries of Tyne and Wear assembled together for the purpose of adopting certain resolutions and considering the best means of obtaining from their employers an increase in wages" (Fynes). Newcastle Town Moor was another favourite. "It was calculated that nearly 200,000 persons had assembled . . . Several speakers addressed the meeting and detailed in homely but energetic language the grievances under which they considered themselves to labour". On 13th August 1831, Fynes tells us: "The miners of the two counties met on Bolden Fell between Gateshead and Sunderland. During the forenoon, the roads in the vicinity presented an unusual bustle, the men walking in procession from different collieries bearing flags and banners and accompanied by bands of music. The banners were numerous and of the gayest description, nearly all being embellished with painted design and with a motto more or less connected with the recent struggle between the miners and employers."

The temper of the gatherings has long trembled the nerves of state authorities, from the time we gathered on the moors fetching fowling-pieces and muskets in the 1800s to the days of 1984 when a miner, from the platform, beseeched the crowds, swelled by the miners of all the counties and countries of Britain in do-or-die action, not to be provoked and to "sleep in ya ain beds the neet, the forces of wor enemies have been arriving here all the week and are camped in prisons, and stationed all round." This is not to say that the Gala has an unbroken thread, characterised by rebellion let alone revolution. The tide of our temper has stamped its dominance upon the occasion, though, of course, never removing minority views, left or right, militant or moderate, as the miners themselves swung to or against dominant Durham leaderships, and their particular political viewpoints. If it is true that for every action there is an equal and positive reaction, just as strong and not just as politically correct, of course, then the platforms and direction of the speakers, followed not long after by portraits on banners and views in the official Gala programme, often reflect it. So the miners' union marched with determined zeal to conflict with the aristocratic coal owners of the early nineteenth century, only to be met by their state in the form of armed soldiers and draconian laws, which dashed the young dreams of liberation. The response was often to seek alternate redress in more moderate aims and leaders. Likewise, the smashing of direct industrial methods of struggle swung the movement into seeking parliamentary redress. So it was that firstly the Liberals and then the Labour Party were seen as the direct agents of the miners' cause. Miners' banners in the age of the Chartists bore such slogans as "Let Those Who Are Without A Sword Sell Their Shirt And Buy One", whilst the 1890s saw more conciliatory pictures of arbitration boards and invitations to the owners "In The Past We Have Been Enemies Now Let Us Be Friends". Likewise, the bitter struggles of the 1920s and the spread of revolutionary ideology produced banners with Marx, Lenin, James Connolly, and slogans in praise of class struggle. As defeat once more wrought havoc to the union and the conditions of the men, more moderate scripts again took dominance. The leaders of the Labour Party with parliamentary aims once more taking up residence, were if not always on top of the radical, at times uneasily alongside.

These changes in mood and character were reflected also in the speaker guest list: Peter Kropotkin (though it is not certain if this was because of his credentials as an Anarchist or his regal lineage as a Russian Prince) or Ramsay MacDonald; Annie Besant or the fiery little MP for Jarrow and

Hetton Lyons Banner 1951

Clem Attlee on balcony - Late 40s

darling of the pit folks, Ellen Wilkinson. Indeed, from the 1930s, and especially through to the 50s and 60s, the Gala platform was the most important political platform for Labour politicians, appearance there was a must. It was a stamp of credibility, and the message put across on that day often forecast changes in policy or leadership challenges.

Pit communities were composites. Mining, until the beginning of this century, was not a skill which allowed the miner or his family to settle long. Frequently, the miner moved from place to place, following the shifts in the fortunes of coal, from expansion to recession, from exhaustion to new winnings. Pit villages were mixtures, and not always comfortable ones, with different pasts and experiences, sometimes different dialects, albeit always pit 'twangs'. The church and chapel, Methodist and Catholic, brought different political and cultural stances, and these, along with the moderate versus revolutionary political strands, were often reflected in crazy mosaic on the banner. It became a custom in some lodges to give the 'sky pilots' the reverse scene and keep the facing scene for the politics. So it was that religious scenes with angels and Jesus brought up the rear while Arthur Cook or Karl Marx led the advance. Few pitmen are ever wholly won to anything and most accepted that there was probably 'something' in both concepts of existence. That the banners should reflect an agnostic pragmatism is entirely in common with the nature of the pitmen themselves. Some will bear the threads from the Chartist era, from the days of the Combination Acts and

Big Meeting 1974

deportation; the all seeing eye that ensures loyalty at times of trial and hardship; the symbols of collectivism over individualism; the tools of our trade; scenes from our lives rarely otherwise witnessed on the surface. Like the magnificent religious costumes of the otherwise totally impoverished Incas, the banner shone like a jewel of silk and gold, whilst many who carried it had felt the pangs of hunger and the chime of the pawn shop. It had to be rich, even if they were not, because the banner itself is a collective aspiration and reflection of their worth. I have seen it carried to dying men's bedsides as final inspiration; carried in churches at funerals; present at christenings; and stuck, as an act defying sacrilege, at the head of strike-breaking collieries, ("Nuw pass this if ye dar").

And what of the folk who follow the banner from the queasy early morning, when the village ring to the incessant thump thump of the bass drum and the first distant notes of the band reach its corners and summon all from their beds for another Big Meeting Day? To them it's another chance to hear the speeches from the platform, to be a little bairn looking at the earnest faces of me Ma and Da as they listen to what prospects for the future of 'our industry', 'our union', 'our movement' and to listen as earnestly in adulthood with our own bairns straining to hear and understand. Then to shout out in anger as the movement dug its moderate heels in, to cheer and weep as militant voices later retook the stage, to turn in disgust as traitors dared face us. But this is more than a political rally, for the young and unattached it has been a place for these last

ninety years or more to funk your stuff, and flaunt the latest fashion. In the 1950s and early 60s, Durham became the biggest assembly of young working-class men and women anywhere, with the exception of the Toon Moor Hoppins. Being unused to viewing the dominant fashion trends of teenage pit folk, a local news cynic dubbed the Gala a Teddy Boy's Picnic! For us, in the late sixties, the day and the age encouraged a mad feeling of abandon and freedom, and skipping teenagers arm-in-arm, rank-on-rank, came to symbolise the joy of the Gala as a whole.

To have lost not only this Coalfield but virtually every other; to feel the consciousness that our great cause is all but run sink deeper and deeper into our collective perception is almost unbearable. This book will mark a movement, retell a story, and, hopefully, help recharge some emerging future force for a change, for freedom, for a brighter world and happier humanity.

Though those with power and privilege, who we dared to challenge, have swept us from the field, the last word is not theirs. They cannot take from us our past and that noble endeavour, nor can they take from us this day, for the Big Meeting is etched in the stone of history thicker than Hadrian's Wall, its memory will live on. The future that our forebears so looked to is still bright, for it is as yet unwritten, and is in our hands and those of our succeeding generations.

Big Meeting 1961

LIST OF GALA DATES AND SPEAKERS 1871 - 1894

1. 1871, August 12th.—Wharton Park, Durham.—Alex. MacDonald, (Glasgow); Wm. Brown (North Staffordshire); J. Normansell (Barnsley); W. Crawford (Sunderland).

2. 1872, June 15th.—Racecourse, Durham—Alex Macdonald (Glasgow); W. Brown (Staffs); Thomas Burt (Newcastle), also Thomas Ramsay; W. Crawford; J. Forman; W. H. Patterson and Nichol Wilkinson.

3. 1873, June 14th.—Joseph Cowen, Alex MacDonald; P. Casey (South Yorks.); Ben Pickard (West Yorks.); Lloyd Jones (London); J. Shepherd (Cleveland); R. Fynes; also W. Crawford and other Agents. There were three platforms.

4. 1874, August 15th.—A. MacDonald; R. Fynes; Mr. Crothier; Lloyd Jones; Charles Bradlaugh; W. Brown (North Staffs.): and Agents.

5. 1875. July 3rd.—Charles Bradlaugh; R. Fynes; Alex MacDonald; T. Burt; Lloyd Jones and Agents.

*This year he N.E.R. withdrew trains so that no person could travel from any stations between Bishop Auckland and Durham, Newcastle and Durham, Lanchester and Durham. Reason given that they could not arrange to transport so many people on a Saturday. In consequence of this, Galas of the two following years were held on Mondays.

6. 1876, July 3rd (Monday.)—A. MacDonald, M.P.; O'Connor Power. M.P.; Lloyd Jones; Mrs. Annie Besant; L. A. Atherley Jones; R. Fynes and William Crawford: John Wilson and Agents.

7. 1877, July 16th (Monday).—Sir Arthur Middleton, M.P.; A. MacDonald, M.P.; L. A. Atherley Jones; T. Burt; W. Brown; R, Fynes; B. Pickard; Mr. O'Neill; J. Toole also T. Ramsay; W. Crawford and other Agents.

8. 1878, July 6th.—A. MacDonald: Farrer Herschell. Q.C., M.P.; R. O'Connor Power. M.P.; Lloyd Jones; R. Fynes: W. Brown; T. Burt: Atherley Jones; Charles Bradlaugh and Agents.

9. 1879. July 5th.—Lloyd Jones; Samuel Stanfield (Ashton-under-Lyme); A. MacDonald, M.P.; R. O'Connor Power, M.P.; T. Burt; L. A. Atherley Jones and Agents.

10. 1880. July 31st.—T. Burt; Charles Bradlaugh; Lloyd Jones: R. Fynes; Ald. J. Fowler and Agents.

11. 1881, July 30th.—Mr. Symes (Birmingham); T. Burt; Charles Bradlaugh; Lloyd Jones and A. MacDonald; also Agents.

12. 1882, July Ist.—Prince Kropotkin: R. O'Connor Power; Lloyd Jones, Joseph Cowen; Charles Bradlaugh.

13. 1883, July 14th.—Joseph Cowen; O'Connor Power; Lloyd Jones; Mayor of Durham, Ald. James Fowler, Chairman.

14. 1884, July 5th.—Charles Bradlaugh; Lloyd Jones; Mrs. Annie Besant; John Morley; T. Burt; Rev. W. Bailey and the Agents.

15. 1885, July 25th.—Ald. J. Fowler; Henry Broadhurst, M.P.; Lloyd Jones; Mr. Bell (Inspector of Mines); Charles Bradlaugh; T. Burt and the Agents.

16. 1886, July 31st.—Charles Bradlaugh; C. Fenwick; Joseph Arch; Rev. R. Hind and the Agents.

17. 1887, July 23rd.—L. A. Atherley Jones; Charles Fenwick; T. Burt; Joseph Arch; Ald. Fowler; R. Fynes and the Agents.

18. 1888, July 14th.—T. Burt, L. A. Atherley Jones; Charles Fenwick; Charles Bradlaugh; Conway, M.P. (North Leitrem); The Mayor of Durham, Dr. Blackett and the Agents.

19. 1889, July 6th.—Rt. Hon. John Morley; T. Burt; Atherley Jones; Ald Fowler and the Agents.

20. 1890, July 12th.—J. Rowland, M.P.; T. D. Sullivan, M.P.; James Joicey, M.P.; Ben Pickard, M.P.; F. S. Stephenson, M.P., and the Agents. (Sir J. Whitwell Pease marched in the ranks of Stanley Lodge).

21. 1891, July 4th.—Mr. Cremer. M.P.; Sam Storey, M.P.; T. Burt, M.P.; L. A. Atherley Jones; also Monsieur Boucher (in England studying).

22. 1892, July 23rd.—J. Havelock Wilson, M.P.; W. Sprow (Seamen's Union); W. Bailey (London); M. Fowler, M.P.; L. A. Atherley Jones, M.P.

23. 1893, July 29th.—Michael Davitt; L. A. Atherley Jones, M.P. Sam Storey, M.P.; J. Havelock Wilson, M.P.

24. 1894, July 21st.—C. Fenwick, M.P.; J. Havelock Wilson, M.P.; John Burns, M.P.; L. A. Atherley Jones, M.P.: Isadore Isaacs (Solicitor to D.M.A.).

Big Meeting 1968

Big Meeting 1950s

THE FIRST BIG MEETING

(extracts from an article in the Durham Miners' Association Gala programme 1966)

Tommy Hepburns grave

"BE NOT WEARY IN WELL-DOING, FOR IN TIME YE SHALL REAP IF YE FAINT NOT."

This noble sentiment was the motto of the Thornley Lodge banner which added a brave splash of colour to the Miners' Gala platform. It was a brilliant day in high summer, and the speakers' enclosure was roofed with a canvas cover to protect its occupants from the blinding heat of the sun. From an early hour miners and their familes had been converging on Durham by road and rail; the morning had been spent sightseeing in and around the city, and as midday approached some five thousand made their way to Wharton Park (loaned for the occasion by John Lloyd Wharton, M.P.) and paid their fee for admission to the first Annual Gala of the Durham Miners' Association.

It was the 12th day of August, 1871, and the Association was a little less than two years old.

If the miners assembled at Wharton Park experienced a sense of satisfaction with their achievements and of pride in the state of their Union, they also realised that much remained to be done. The first fruits of their labours were almost within their grasp: within the next twelve months the bond was to be abolished for ever, its place taken by fortnightly contracts; a Joint Committee of Owners' and Workmen's representatives was to be set up for the negotiation of wages and conditions and the settlement of disputes; the Mines Regulation Act was to be passed, providing amongst other measures that no boy under 10 years of age should be employed in any coalmine, that boys of between 12 and 13 should attend school for at least 20 hours in a fortnight, that wages should not be paid in public houses, that coal should be paid for by weight, the men to have the right to appoint and pay a check-weighman, that no person should be employed in any mine without a second shaft or outlet. Every mine manager was to be a qualified mining engineer, safety and ventilation regulations were laid down and provision was made for proper inspections by Government Inspectors. Within five years they were to have their own Headquarters, a splendid Council Chamber and office block in Durham's North Road.

A long, hard and tortuous road lay ahead of the Union, but already to those early pioneers the milestones of victory were in sight as they crowded expectantly around the platform in Wharton Park.

The chair was taken (as it is to this day) at "twelve o'clock to the minute." Mr. Crawford's first words as Chairman were "This is the first great Gala Day of the Durham Miners' Mutual Confident Association, and I only pray that it will not be the last. I can assure you that on this, the twelfth day of August, 1871, the Durham Miners' Association was never in a more healthy position; never more healthy with regard to its feelings and determination to carry on its great work of organising the county; never more healthy with respect to its funds; never more healthy in reference to the general progressive tendency of its operations, since the first day the Association was established."

The long, hot day wore on. Large numbers took tea in the Long Room at the park, and others patronised the refreshment tent run by Mr. George Oswald of the Market Hotel, which was one of the principal meeting places of the Union's Committees and where in fact the Union officially came into being.

The shadows lengthened; the last of the bands had marched away; the victors of the sports arena had departed; preparations were made for the long journey home. The first Gala was over.

WORKING MEN

Think what power lies within you,
For what triumphs you were formed;
Think, but not alone of living
Like the horse from day to day;
Think, but not alone of giving
Health for self, and soul for pay.
Think! Oh be machines no longer,
Engines made of flesh and blood;
Thought will make you fresher, stronger,
Link you to the great and good.
Thought is as a wand of power,
Power to make oppression shrink;
Grasp ye then the precious dower,
Poise it, wield it, work and think!

William Brown
*(recited at the end of the first Gala in
Wharton Park, 1871)*

Racecourse 1950

Kibblesworth Band returning from Durham, 1903

photo Beamish Museum

COMING FOR THEIR REETS

(extracts from an article in the Durham Miners' Association Centenary Gala programme 1966)

On a night in August 1871 the denizens of the fair City of Durham had an uneasy time of it. They had prepared themselves for the morrow as if for a siege. Doors were bolted, windows barred, and children sent to bed with stories of the barbarians who were coming for their 'reets'. Twenty years later John Wilson recalled the day in vivid fashion. "The approach of the ruthless Goth upon the ancient city of Rome filling, as it did, the inhabitants with terror and dismay, was no more alarming than was the knowledge that the miners were about to hold their first Gala in Durham". This gathering was a direct result of a resolution that the DMA Council should take into consideration the desirability of holding a general meeting of miners in the central district.

It is evident that those infant meetings were rallying points: in fact later Rules refer to the Annual Demonstration. The Association was young, insecure, and needed a base from which to proclaim its policies and increase its membership. It had been tried before. On Wednesday, April 6th, 1831, large bodies of colliers passed through Newcastle to Black Fell, bearing banners with words like "Order" and "Unity" inscribed on them. A fortnight later there was another assembly at Jarrow, and colliery names were on the banners borne by groups of men. Lumley Colliery had this biblical reference—"Stand fast therefore in the liberty wherewith Christ hath made you free, and be not entangled with the yoke of bondage". A direct reference to the infamous Bond which made pitmen the chattels of a privileged few.

Workers had discovered the devices of banners and were finding them to be a supreme expression of their convictions and a means of "floating" their mottoes for all to see—visual aids, in modern parlance.

The early primitive banners were soon to be replaced. At about this time George Tutill, a young showman from Hull, was travelling the fairground circuit. Of artistic temperament and with a high degree of business acumen, Tutill realised the potential for well-designed banners. The paintings of the booths, a century or so removed from baroque styling, undoubtedly configured in early banner design. Tutill established his business in 1837 and the banners of the Durham miners, with few exceptions, were made, repaired, and altered by this firm for over a century. They have depicted religious

17

themes, political dogma and the faces of famous leaders. The faggot, the wheatsheaf and the widow's mite were to be seen flapping on canvas along with portraits of Union pioneers and political prodigies of the Lib-Lab and the Labour representation organisation. These were the beginnings of a meeting of workers which has become world famous: the Big Meeting or Gayla or Gahla Day, however you choose to pronounce it.

What is true is that each Gala has a cache of memories for someone, and one or two of the meetings have given rise to powerful emotions and stirring events. Even though 1871 is recorded as the first meeting, John Wilson always referred to the Gala of 1872 as the beginning of the Big Meeting. The Borough Magistrates needed some persuading to issue the licences to the refreshment booths. William Crawford was very persuasive— "For our own part, we have not the slightest doubt of the proceedings being characterised by anything but the best of feeling and order on the part of the men engaging in the demonstration, which we are sure is intended to partake more of the character of a monster 'outing' of a class of men whose only desire is to discuss amongst themselves the best means of improving, in a rational and legal manner, their condition, rather than an assemblage of either political or social conspirators and agitators. Almost the worse contingency, however, has been anticipated, as there will be a force of 40 policemen on the ground, the expense of the attendance of 20 of whom will be borne by the Miners' Association, whilst the remuneration of the remaining 20 will be defrayed from the funds of the borough watch rate". Some people wanted soldiers in readiness but the Mayor, Mr. J. Fowler, allayed their doubts—"I know the pitmen better than you, and there is no fear".

Resolutions from the gathering were sent to the Prime Minister and the Home Secretary. They expressed satisfaction at the improvement in the affairs of the DMA, both numerically and financially, took umbrage with the amendments to the Payment of Wages Bill, affirmed that the Durham miners wanted to retain weekly wage payments, looked askance at the Criminal Law Amendment Act of 1871, and agreed that the principle of arbitration was a logical way of settling differences between employer and employed.

The banners were displayed in prominent and pleasing fashion at the 1872 demonstration. Over 70 flags ranged round the boundary of the field close to the water's edge, with the platform erected at the opposite perimeter. In picture form the beehive of production ran counter to the bosses who stole the honey; the faggot displayed its principle of binding and strength, and arbitration, compensation, education and wel-

Ryhope Lodge preparing for Durham 1908   *photo Beamish Museum*

fare were recurrent themes. Byer Moor had an unusually trenchant word or two on trade:

Our masters they do tell us
That if we mean to stand
We shall do ourselves an injury
And the trade will leave the land.
But in that we have advantage
And that you know is true
For if the trade leaves England
We can leave it too.

In 1923 the Dean of Durham, Dr. J. E. C. Welldon, was rescued from a ducking in the Wear by a prescient oarsman who had pulled his boat in not far from where the huge man was being jostled by a crowd of angry miners. The men had confused him with the Bishop of Durham, Dr. H. Hensley Henson—a man who would have gone into Welldon's pocket. The intrepid Bishop had criticised the Labour County Council of Durham for 'unexampled extravagance' in laying down six miles of new road between Durham and Lanchester, using local labour—some of the labourers being former miners out of work through the depression.

The story ends with a butler bringing the ruffled Dean a glass of still lemonade on a silver tray. It is a motley tale of two bishops and two years (1925 is mentioned).

The Gala is essentially a light-hearted occasion, and there are no extant records of those years when sorrow struck; until 1951, when a solitary banner was borne silently over the crowded streets. There was no band, no fuss, just a banner draped in black: the cynosure of a thousand eyes. Easington had come to pay its respects to the dead of

photo Beamish Museum   *Deaf Hill Band & Banner 1924*

the village. The hushed crowd regarded the sombre banner with bared heads, muffled cheers and a sorrowing silence. Some wept openly. Others fondled the cloth as if trying to shake the hands of those who had been torn from them. And not far away were the widow drapes of Eppleton— two disasters in one year. Before the speakers had their say, the tragic tones of 'Gresford' told of sorrows bravely borne. Gresford, the Welsh mining disaster of the thirties so poignantly remembered through the composition of Robert Saint, a Hebburn miner who devoted

his life to the cause of pit ponies.

By 1966 the number of banners ensconced on the racecourse had dwindled to 63 and 1970, the end of the Robens' ten-year stint, witnessed two invited speakers and one platform. Would it end not with a bang but a whimper? Not likely. 1969 was the centenary year of the Durham Miners' Association and just before the Gala the late Joseph Stubs of Toft Hill remarked to Sid Chaplin that "there is nothing I would like to see better at this year's Gala than some of the old banners brought out on parade or ringed round the racecourse, just as they used to be." Joe had his wish fulfilled. Nearly 30 banners were brought out of their 'coffins' and paraded behind the Handon Hold band, "resurrected" for the occasion. It was a Gala of ghosts and memories.

No matter how we regard the figure of a Bishop on what amounts to a political platform, the Cathedral service has been a part of Gala affairs since 1897, and the men and boys who have died in the pits of Durham are remembered in the Mother Church. A skilfully carved black Spanish Mahogany fireplace is their memorial. For many years it was lodged at Ramside Hall, and was

given to the Cathedral by the Pemberton family whose name was initially borne by Wearmouth Colliery.

The memorial was assembled by the craftsmen of the Dean and Chapter and the centre panel bears a representation in gilt of a Davy Lamp with the words:

REMEMBER BEFORE GOD THE DURHAM MINERS WHO HAVE GIVEN THEIR LIVES IN THE PITS OF THIS COUNTY, AND THOSE WHO WORK IN DARKNESS AND DANGER IN THOSE PITS TODAY.

Paradoxically, beneath the dedicatory sentence there are words taken from Job 28 v 4:

He breaketh open the shaft from where men sojourn; they are forgotten by the foot that passeth by.

The dedication service which was performed by the Bishop of Durham, Dr. Alwyn Williams, took place on Saturday, February 22nd, 1947, whilst one of the worst blizzards for half a century raged round the stalwart cathedral.

Politicians have made their own assessment of the meeting, and there is no better analogy than Nye Bevan's piquant remark —"I saw A. J. Cook's portrait alongside that of Peter Lee—they used to quarrel like Kilkenny cats. Now they are on the same banner—and they are silent. They are no longer quarrelling. Why! Only because they are dead."

In 1935 Hannen Swaffer was penning his idiosyncratic view of our Gala for the Daily Herald—"The banners were a defiant symbol of their determination to establish, one day, social justice—the bands a proud sign of their long struggle for a culture denied them in the schools. And so there passed out of Durham, for another year of toil, or unemployment, the army of the miners, whom 'Civilisation' treats as slaves, although they are the salt of the earth."

Some say the Gala is dead. Long live the Gala.

Durham Cathedral

REMEMBER BEFORE GOD THE DURHAM MINERS WHO HAVE GIVEN THEIR LIVES IN THE PITS OF THIS COUNTY AND THOSE WHO WORK IN DARKNESS AND DANGER IN THOSE PITS TODAY

HE BREAKETH OPEN A SHAFT AWAY FROM WHERE MEN SOJOURN THEY ARE FORGOTTEN OF THE FOOT THAT PASSETH BY. JOB 28.4.

photo Tony Whittle

Bearpark Lodge 1981

LIST OF GALA DATES AND SPEAKERS 1895 - 1925

25. 1895, July 27th.—Sam Storey, M.P., John Burns, M.P.; 1. Burt. M.P.; C. Fenwick, M.P.; J. Havelock Wilson, M.P.;

26. 1896, July 18th.—Robert Cameron, M.P.; J. Havelock Wilson, M.P.; M. Fowler, M.P.; L. A. Atherley Jones, M.P.; Sam Storey, M.P.

27. 1897, July 24th.—T. Mann, Joseph Hopper, L. A. Atherley Jones, M.P.; J. Havelock Wilson, M.P.; Robert Cameron, M.P.; M. Fowler, M.P.

28. 1898, July 16th.—J. Havelock Wilson, M.P.; S. Storey, M.P. T. Mann; Robert Cameron, M.P.; John Coward.

29. 1899, July 22nd.—Canon Moore Ede; T. Mann; C. Fenwick, M.P.; E. Rhymer (Barnsley); S. Storey, M.P.; J. Havelock Wilson, M.P.; Ald. C. Rowlandson; Mayor of Durham (Coun. W. Gray).

30. 1900, July 28th.—Tom Mann; L. A. Atherley Jones, M.P.; John Burns, M.P.: J. Havelock Wilson.

31. 1901, July 20th.—J. H. Wilson; Sam Storey; Tom Mann; L. A. Atherley Jones, M.P.

32. 1902, July 26th.—John Burns, M.P.; J. H. Wilson; L. A. Atherley Jones, M.P.; W. H. Thompson (Editor of Reynolds).

33. 1903, July 18th.—Canon Moore Ede, Will Crooks, M.P.; W. H. Thompson; (John Burns, M.P., unable to come).

34. 1904, July 23rd—John Burns, M.P.; J. H. Wilson; Will Crooks, M.P.; Canon Moore Ede; W. H. Thompson (Editor Reynolds); Mr. Scaife (U.S.A.).

35. 1905 July 29th.—A. Henderson, M.P.; Keir Hardie, M.P.; Will Crooks, M.P.; W. H. Thompson (Editor Reynolds).

36. 1906, July 21st.—J. H. Wilson; J. Keir Hardie, M.P.; Philip Snowden, M.P.; John Ward, M.P.; T. MacKnight (nearly 102 years old from Haswell Homes).

37. 1907, July 27th.—Philip Snowden, M.P.; Arthur Henderson, M.P.; Will Crooks, M.P.; J. H. Wilson; Canon Moore Ede.

38. 1908, July 18th.—A. Henderson, M.P.; Philip Snowden, M.P.; J. Ward, M.P.; J. H. Wilson.

39. 1909, July 24th.—T. P. O'Connor, M.P.; C. Fenwick, M.P.; Victor Grayson, M.P.; Will Crooks, M.P.; J. Wood (Pennsylvania).

40. 1910, August 13th.—J. Keir Hardie, M.P.; Philip Snowden, M.P.; George N. Barnes, M.P.; A. Henderson, M.P.; The Mayor of Durham, W. H. Wood.

41. 1911, July 22nd.—Evan Hayward, W. Crooks, M.P.; Victor Grayson, M.P.; Robert Smillie; Mr. Bowman (M.P. Queensland, Australia).

42. 1912, July 27th.—George Lansbury, M.P.; T. Mann; T. Richardson, M.P.; James Ramsay MacDonald, M.P.; Dean of Worcester and Mrs. Moore Ede; Rev. J. R. Croft.

43. 1913, July 18th.—Evan Hayward, M.P.; J. M. Robertson, M.P.; Stephen Walsh, M.P.; Arthur Henderson, M.P., Dr. J. R. Harker, U.S.A.

44. 1914, July 25th.—T. Richardson, M.P.; Robert Smillie, M.P.; Jim Larkin; J. Ramsay MacDonald, M.P.; Dean of Worcester, (Moore Ede).

1915
1916
1917
1918 War Period—No Gala held.

45. 1919, July 26th.—Sir Leo Chiozza Money: Robert Smillie, Esq. President, Miners' Federation of Great Britain; Rt. Hon. J. R. Clynes, M.P.; F. Hodges, Esq., Secretary, Miners' Federation of Great Britain.

46. 1920, July 27th.—Ernest Bevin; Philip Snowden; George Lansbury; W. R. Fairley; Dean of Worcester; Mayor of Durham (Coun. W. H. Wood).

1921. None held. National Lock-out.

1922. None held. Depression after Lock-out.

47. 1923, July 28th.—J. Ramsay MacDonald, M.P.; Rev. H. Dunnico, M.P.; Frank Hodges; Jack Jones, M.P.

48. 1924, July 19th.—Robert Smillie; J. J. Lawson, M.P.; George Lansbury, M.P.; James Welsh, M.P.

49. 1925, July 25th.—J. Ramsay MacDonald, M.P.; E. Shinwell; Sir Patrick Hastings, M.P.; Margaret Bondfield, M.P.

1926. None held.—National Lock-out.

50. 1927, August 13th.—Jack Jones, M.P.; A. J. Cook; Oswald Mosley, M.P.; Ellen Wilkinson, M.P.

51. 1928, July 28th.—E. Shinwell; D. Kirkwood, M.P.; James Maxton, M.P.; S. Satlatvala, M.P.; Dean of Worcester.

52. 1929, July 27th.—Ellen Wilkinson, M.P.; A. J. Cook; Oswald Mosley, M.P.; Jennie Lee, M.P.

photo Beamish Museum

Philadelphia Lodge 1950

23

photo Northern Echo

Big Meeting 1957

Gaitskell and Robens on Balcony 1958

photo T. Smith   *Kelloe Lodge setting off for Durham*

WOR BIG MEETING

The morn is wor Big Meetin' day,
The grandest day of aal.
The banner lifts at 8 o'clock
Ootside the Miners' Haal.
Wor lass and bairns'll aal be there
And Granny in her shaal.

We'll march through Durham's coggley streets
To music from wor band,
Wi' croods in front and croods ahint
And croods on eethor hand.
And on wor backs'll be the bairns,
The bonniest in the land.

The speakin' starts at half past eleven
We'll hear wor Arthur's pattor,
He'll talk aboot the Government
Or some such vital mattor,
And if he disen't please us, why
We'll hoy him in the wattor.

And when the speechifyin's done,
And all the Nobs hev went,
We'll find a seat and hev wor bait
In the aad Esh Winnin' tent,
Then join the folks aroond the shows
That's aal on pleasure bent.

Back in the toon we'll tak a drink
And flirt wi' all the lasses,
And spare a word for aal we meet,
Aal kinds, aal creeds, aal classes.
But canny on, me bonny lads
And divven't smash the glasses.

And, as the darkness cums to end
This best of aal good neets,
We'll climb the hill and leave behind
The friendly, homely streets.
And, though we're tired and footsore, why
At least we've had wor reets!   *(Anonymous)*

27

THE DAY ALL GLORY UNFURLED

by the late Sid Chaplin
(reproduced from the 1983 Northern Echo
Centenary Gala supplement)

Born in 1916, just three years after the British coal industry achieved its peak bulk output, I grew up in time to see the first convulsive death-throes of Durham as a great coal-exporting coalfield. Not that I ever saw it that way.

To me, all seemed largely pits and pit villages, set against which hills, fields and river - together with clouds, continually scudding eastwards - constituted little more than a perpetual scenic backdrop.

At every journey's end was a pit, and pits were all important, particularly your own: Shildon, Westerton, Byers Green, Newfield and Dean and Chapter (in all of which my father worked) were in turn the be-all and end-all of life.

Those men who didn't have a nickname were known by their pit job; and how they did it established their rank in the community. The pit regulated not only all the men's comings and goings but the life and being of every soul in the village, whether man, woman or child.

And the pit was an entity, loved as well as hated. I still recall how shattered my grandfather was when they closed Shildon Lodge.

Sid Chaplin left

North of England Newspapers

New Shildon Lodge 1964

But normally the pit was the real core of the village. That piston-beat of the winder which went on at Thornley to the end was symbolical of the heart of every Durham tribe. Even when lads were conscious at school that real education was for pit-work.

Individual though my first pit may have been with its tall window house so like a Borderer's pele tower and its wooden head-gear, its boilers hissing steam and its row upon row of beehive cooking ovens so near the Bishop Auckland highway that it was safer to cross the road when one of those enormous brick kilns was discharging its white-hot load, it was the Lodge banner - its virtual embodiment - that left the most lasting mark upon me.

At another time and place I crystallised just how seminal this first glimpse of identity proved to be for a child not yet five years of age:

"Black was the first pit I knew; its heapstead and pulleys and the muck around, black as on old sow's back. By day she swallowed up clean laughing lads and men, only to disgorge them black and bone-weary in the evening. But larks sang the day they hoisted the banner and to my childish mind it was the loveliest sight in all Creation when, with a sharp flap, the picture billowed and sailed away."

, Oddly enough, after my first meeting with a banner, I took little notice of the many other banners that came my way.

This may been due to the sheer size of that glorious colouring of that first banner - more than 50 years later I walked straight up to it in the DLI exhibition, although the leading (named) side was not exhibited.

It wasn't the picture so much (The Good Samaritan) as the memory of the colours, still miraculously preserved, if somewhat faded, which led me homing straight to it. This was the Westerton banner.

The others I hardly noticed (not in detail, anyway), and I can only suppose that boy-like, I was more attracted to the bands. No banner is complete without a brass or silver band. But, now that I think of it, the banner was there all the time, essential if now no more that a commonplace.

And so too were the pits. Pits were everywhere then. Although our own was hidden, we continually heard the clash of its screens, and the clank of its tankie engine. Over the brow of the hill was Byers Green, to which it was joined underground.

On a clear day you could see - and hear - a whole ring of pits, all the way from Bishop Auckland to Brancepeth and beyond - the pits of the Wear Valley.

In the early morning you could hear the staccato beat of their winding exhaust pipes, the whir of their ventilation fans and the sharp shouts of the lads driving their ponies and loaded stone tubs along the long low ridges of the faraway pit heaps - many a plume of smoke too, as coal trains snaked down the colliery lines to the LNER.

Slowly I entered my wider heritage. At six I found the immense sands, the pounding sea, at Seaton Carew, and saw by the Tees the night sky light up and the yellow smoke billowing - and no one told me that the blastfurnaces were fed with coking coal from home.

At ten I stayed with an aunt along a nar-row passageway in Old Elvet in Durham.

Three things I remember. Turning from the Cathedral's reflection in the river and seeing the high pinnacles in all their solidity, shiver then settle again. My aunt with a raised finger "when that clock strikes eight again a man will have been hanged." Slim boats turning like water-spiders below Prebend's Bridge while spray revealed that it wasn't glass but a flow that went thunderously over the weir.

Years later I spent my last shilling going up the great tower and walked six miles home haunted by the men shuffling round the prison yard. The erratic jackdaws, the levitating gulls, the crystal air had cried out insult. We were glad to escape and scamper down a winding street to see the bands and banners march out again.

What a day! We had heard Wee Ellen Wilkinson and C. R. Attlee speaking - flaming youth and calm cool maturity both bearing out the truth of St. Paul's dictum that all things are possible through faith.

Naturally, Wee Ellen was our pin-up while the little Captain seemed something of an oddity. Who would have guessed then that in little more than a decade this dry little man would head the greatest reforming government in British history!

In the full neaptide of Durham coal probably more than 300 banners paraded. Little more than 30 years ago there were 200. I arrived at my first Big Meeting about 50 years ago on the eight o'clock train from Ferryhill to find the first banners away. The last banner marched past the County Hotel at noon: I should know as I marched behind it.

Big Meeting 1950s

H. Wilson 1963 Gala

Dancing on Racecourse   photo Beamish Museum

Admittedly, the crowds are thinner and the intervals between the banners grow progressively longer (what a pity, one often thinks, that the mechanised face teams operating machines which shear through the coal, cutting and loading ten tonnes a minute, can't be invited complete with their own bannerettes to march behind the various home banners); but then the Gala, which long ago began as a demonstration, has now evolved into a family gathering.

Many like myself who have left the coal, return again and again to meet old marrers and thousands who now work in the deep pits of South Yorkshire, the Midlands, and South Wales wouldn't miss the great reunions for worlds.

And this year's bright idea of augmenting the banners of the working collieries by the "fostering" of historical lodge banners carried by DMA volunteers, and also inviting along Lodges (together with their bands and banners) from Northumberland, Yorkshire and South Wales, must still further engender the larger family spirit while at the same time reviving to a degree the great drawing power of thousands of pitmen and their wives and families marching peacefully for their ideals and aspirations.

All the more so now that we may now be confronted with a 1930s kind of situation again, together with the need for painful rethinking and rebuilding.

Nearly 80 years ago my old friend the late Joseph Stubbs came to his first Big Meeting with his Da, who lifted the eight-year-old laddie on his shoulders. "Now sing out the names on the banners, my lad!"

And a few minutes later when young Jos yelled out, "Here's Black Prince, Tow Law, Da!" the two fell in behind. The father, just then painfully learning to read, depended on his son to find his old workmates, who had moved on to the other pit.

Incidentally, this was one occasion when a coalminers' Lodge was played in by a leadminers' band - Rookhope lads, they had left home at four a.m. that Saturday and wouldn't get back till five the following morning - 25 hours on their feet and all for five bob a man!

In the old days every Lodge struck its own Union medal which the wives stitched into their husbands' jacket lapels, so that every man marched under his own banner wearing the Lodge medal, rank after rank with the sun glinting on the bronze.

It was different in the Thirties when I first went along to hear Jimmy Maxton and Wee Ellen Wilkinson; all too often the best blue Sunday suits of men marching four abreast were shiny with age. But how those 24in. bottoms flapped!

Then it was understood that everybody marched in - the dancing under the banners was kept for the march out. And the marchers of the morning came in marching four deep with almost military precision - yet without a hint of militarism.

The bonniest sight I ever saw was from the topmost room of the Castle. There, far below, the smooth glissade of water swept between the piers of Framwellgate Bridge, while counterwise on the road above, pent within the narrow walls went the other great flow of people. The banners came close and gay, all aglow in scarlet, gold and royal blue, each preceded by rank after rank of shining brass.

Mind you, the job of banner-carrier is no sinecure. Even in a slight breeze the great embroidered silken squares billow and pull like sails. Caught by a high wind in the narrow funnel of Silver Street, they pitch and toss like ships in a storm. The stout poles transformed into live things with an impulse to lift off vertically can make bairns of brawny six footers, wrestle as they will. Banners before now have rent asunder.

As works of art the banners may be negligible. To me they are the most beautiful creations in all the world, and have been ever since the day when my Uncle Edward lifted me on to his shoulder to see Westerton's unfurled and played away. Although I was only four, the glory of that day is still with me.

Their massed effect, of course, is terrific, either in swaying motion or spread out in proud array on the racecourse; but for mining folk they represent more than a mere spectacle.

Here trysts were made and kept and later husbands met their wives and bonny bairns for a picnic in their shade, while veterans re-fought old battles with recalcitrant managers, or shifted (in retrospect) enough coal to keep every family on the field warm for the rest of their lives. The banners are at once the roof-tree of the mining family and the standards of the regiments of coal.

From some flutter a length of crepe in token that one who marched last year will march no more. And there are other invisible battle honours, the banners commemorate generations of miners who rode down into the depths on a rope as heavy with men and boys as the vine with fruit; men who lost their grip and fell, or were crushed in the vine-press of the stratum, or were blasted to oblivion in the searing flame of firedamp.

Seven Jarrow pitmen were transported to Botany Bay and another was gibbeted higher than Haman over Jarrow Slake to crush the spirit of the rest, but they rose again and again. The first leader of the Durham miners to win them recognition had slept when a child in a hedge, just one victim of the mass evictions which were a commonplace of the early strikes.

It is a triumph that the Durham miner of today, after three centuries of deep-mining, has pushed out the frontiers of the Coalfield almost five miles undersea, to break production records. But his finest achievement is the sense of family and kinship he has built up and maintained with irrepressible gaiety and wit.

And it's the unrepentant mixture of fun and seriousness, of re-union and celebration, which makes the Big Meeting the event in the calendar it is.

If the speeches are dull (and dull they can be) there are arguments in plenty to be had with the volatile young rebels whose purpose it is to resurrect Kropotkin or to bring back old Trotsky. With more than the usual quota of razor-sharp minds among the passing multitude they often get as good as they give.

Beer flows in cataracts and churches and chapels set all their good ladies working to provide their traditional ham and pease-pudding teas, unless your prefer to eat your hot-dog walking.

The showfolk are hard at it, on one of the biggest days of their year, and those as get tired of paying for a while can find a lass and dance to the music of folk groups, or the jazz and pop sections of the resting brass. There is jousting in boats on the river.

And away up in the Cathedral the great doors are thrown open and selected bands process in solemn procession. The moment is most solemn. There is a rustle as the vast congregation rises with one accord. St. Cuthbert's folk have come to pay their respects again.

LIST OF GALA DATES AND SPEAKERS 1930 - 1957

53. 1930, July 26th.—Ernest Bevin; A. Shepherd, M.P.; Rt. Hon. William Graham, M.P. (President, Board of Trade); Rt. Hon. George Lansbury, M.P. (J. Ramsay MacDonald and A. J. Cook unable to attend).

54. 1931, July 25th.—E. Shinwell, M.P.; Rev. Herbert Dunnico, M.P.; James Maxton, M.P.; A. J. Cook.

55. 1932, July 23rd.—Tom Johnson, M.P. (Scotland); Jennie Lee; George Lansbury, M.P.; Ebby Edwards.

56. 1933, July 22nd.—Rt. Hon. Arthur Greenwood, M.P.; Hannen Swaffer, Rt. Hon. Herbert Morrison, George Lansbury, M.P.

57. 1934, July 28th.—C. R. Atlee, M.P.; Ebby Edwards; Professor H. Laski; Ellen Wilkinson.

58. 1935, July 27th.—Sir Stafford Cripps, M.P.; Hannen Swaffer; Rt. Hon. Herbert Morrison; George Lansbury, M.P.

59. 1936, July 25th.—Joseph Jones; Rt. Hon. Arthur Greenwood, M.P; Major C. R. Attlee, M.P.; E. Shinwell, M.P.

60. 1937, July 24th.—Rt. Hon. H. Morrison, M.P.; Professor H. Laski; Sir Stafford Cripps, M.P. (and Lady Cripps); Ebby Edwards.

61. 1938, July 23rd—George Lansbury, M.P.; C. R. Attlee, M.P.; Rt. Hon. A. Greenwood, M.P.; Joseph Jones; also visitors, Alexei Nikolenko, President Don-bas Miners, U.S.S.R., and Dr. Camps, a lady from Spain.

62. 1939, July.—Sir Stafford Cripps, M.P.; Mr. Aneurin Bevan, M.P.; Ebby Edwards; and Rt. Hon. H. Morrison, M.P.

1940
1941
1942
1943
1945   War Period - No Gala held.

63. 1946, July 20th.—Rt. Hon. Clem Attlee. M.P., Prime Minister; Rt. Hon. Aneurin Bevan, M.P., Minister of Health; Rt. Hon. Hugh Dalton, M.P., Chancellor of the Exchequer; Ebby Edwards, Secretary of the National Union of Mineworkers.

64. 1947, July 26th.—Rt. Hon. Ernest Bevin, M.P., Foreign Secretary; Rt. Hon. Herbert Morrison, M.P., Lord President of the Council; Michael Foot, M.P.; A. L. Horner, Secretary of the National Union of Mineworkers.

65. 1948, July 24th. Rt. Hon. Sir Hartley Shawcross, K.C., M.P.. Attorney General; Rt. Hon. Sir Stafford Cripps, K.C., M.P., Chancellor of the Exchequer; Rt. Hon. A. Bevan, M.P., Minister of Health; A. L. Horner, General Secretary, National Union of Mineworkers.

66. 1949, July 23rd.—Rt. Hon. Clem, Attlee, C.H., M.P., Prime Minister; Rt. Hon. Ernest Bevin. M.P., Foreign Secretary; Rt. Hon. Herbert Morrison, M.P., Lord President of the Council; A. L. Horner, Esq., General Secretary. National Union of Mineworkers.

67. 1950, July 22nd.—Rt. Hon. Sir Hartley Shawcross, K.C., M.P., Attorney General; Rt. Hon. A. Bevan, M.P., Minister of Health; Rt. Hon. E. Shinwell, M.P., Secretary of State for War; A. L. Horner, Esq., General Secretary, National Union of Mineworkers.

68. 1951, July 21st.—The Rt. Hon. C. R. Attlee, C.H., M.P., Prime Minister; The Rt. Hon. H. Morrison, M.P., Foreign Secretary; Michael Foot, Esq., M.P.; A. L. Horner, Esq., Secretary, National Union of Mineworkers.

69. 1952, July 26th.—The Rt. Hon. Aneurin Bevan, M.P.; The Rt. Hon. Sir Hartley Shawcross, Q.C., M.P.; Miss Margaret Herbison, M.P.; A. L. Horner, Esq., Secretary, National Union of Mineworkers.

70. 1953, July 18th.—The Rt. Hon. C. R. Attlee, C.H., M.P.; The Rt. Hon. Herbert Morrison, M.P.; Mrs. Barbara Castle, M.P.; A. L. Horner, Esq., Secretary, National Union of Mineworkers.

71. 1954, July 17th.—The Rt. Hon. Sir Hartley Shawcross, Q.C., M.P.; The Rt. Hon. Aneurin Bevan, M.P.; Mrs. Bessie Braddock, M.P.; A. L. Horner, Esq., Secretary, National Union of Mineworkers.

72. 1955, July 16th.—The Rt. Hon. C. R. Attlee, O.M., C.H., M.P.; The Rt. Hon, H. T. N. Gaitskell, M.P., Michael Foot, Esq., A. I.. Horner, Esq., Secretary, National Union of Mineworkers.

73. 1956, July 21st.—R. H. S. Crossman, M.P.; L. J. Callaghan, M.P.; R. W. Williams, M.P.; A. L. Horner, Esq., Secretary. National Union of Mineworkers.

74. 1957, July 20th.—A. W. J. Greenwood, M.P.; T. F. Peart, M.P.; W. R. Blyton, M.P.; A. L. Horner, Esq., Secretary, National Union of Mineworkers.

Banners on Racecourse 1950

Big Meeting pre-war

Morrison Busty Lodge 1973

THE PROLETARIAN DISPLAY

Previously unpublished extract by Rough Lea-born novelist Harry Heslop (1898-1983)

When Bob Smillie and Chiozza Money came to address the first Durham Gala after the war, we carried our banners and escorted our brass bands with the deepest of reverence. In those days, the Gala was a sight for all men to witness. The enormity of the proceedings outstripped the imagination. Perhaps it was the setting that lent privilege to the proletarian display. Maybe the vast mustering of the colliery tribes, under the arches of the massive, brick-built viaduct that spans the yonder part of the city and carries the great railway, grants a piquancy to the subsequent proceedings. The boomings of the drums provoking the attention of the tribes and then the double tap which unleashes the brazen sound into an almost dreamlike unreality and sets men and women marching. Repeated almost two hundred times the resultant noise and slashings of colour provoke an almost spiritual aura that hangs like a proud destiny over the immense beauty and the rich colour of the city.

The narrow streets forced an intermingling of marchers and amused watchers. The crossing of the bridge over the Wear, that cowers like a coward within the ample shade of the great cliff that holds both Castle and Cathedral up to the arms of God, was always a strain lain upon the carriers of the banners. The passing over the bridge, beneath the lovely scene evoked by tree-clad heights and glory-crowned buildings, always evoked for me some strangely murmured benediction wailing softly into unreality. There is nothing so magnificent within Christendom that compares with the loveliness of Durham Cathedral. Ordinary men must have built it but they must have been men filled with an extraordinary vision, for they left it, where it stands, encompassing, and encompassed by, its own earth rising upwards to immortality like a prayer passing the lips of a woman suckling her babe.

It is this Cathedral which has softened the harsh lines of the men of coal every time they have ventured into the city to listen to the orators. It is never forbidding, never minatory. It watches them marching to their venue, and when all is over, it beckons them back to their possession of their own lives. It is this half-church, half-refuge, that softens the spirit after the pains of unremitting toil and tempers the thunderings of exhortation into croonings and beliefs.

Leo Chiozza Money removed his hat and stood up to speak to us on that day. The Gala had been a revelation to him, to such a degree that he was still astonished and bewildered. Bob Smillie sat smiling. Both had been fighters at the hearings of the Sankey Commission. Bob could understand the little man's bewilderment. And when Money had breathed his prayer over the vast crowd, "God bless you all," Bob reached over and patted him on the shoulder. Bob was a showman in his own right. He stood up and accepted the acclamations of the concourse. While it boomed over the city, and stilled the rowers in the boats on the lovely breast of the Wear that flowed nearby, he mounted a chair and when the noise had died away he began to speak.

DURHAM BIG MEETIN' DAY

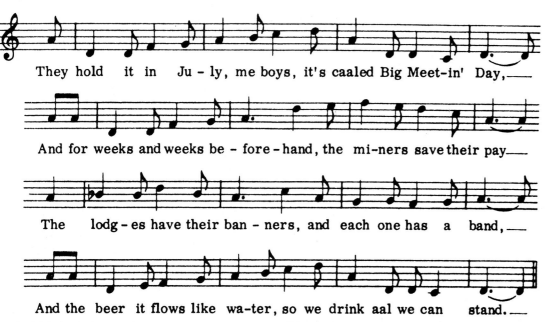

They hold it in Ju - ly, me boys, it's caaled Big Meet-in' Day,——

And for weeks and weeks be - fore-hand, the mi-ners save their pay——

The lodg - es have their ban - ners, and each one has a band,——

And the beer it flows like wa-ter, so we drink aal we can stand.——

They hold it in July, me boys, it's caaled Big Meetin' Day,
And for weeks and weeks beforehand, the miners save their pay.
The lodges have their banners, and each one has a band,
And the beer it flows like water, so we drink aal we can stand.

The polises close the roads up, they torn the cars away
For Durham is stoppened off, me lads, upon Big Meetin' Day.
The bandsmen aal assemble with their horns so blindin' bright,
And they blaa from in the mornin' till gannin' hyem at night.

The crowds they aal gather an' the bands begin te play.
They march up to the Meetin' groond, an' Ryhope leads the way,
An' then we hear the speeches, an' they tell us what gans on,
Of wor hopes an' troubles, an' where the government's gannin' wrong.

Noo, as they speak o present times, me mind it wanders back
To work an' unions long ago when masters broke yer back.
Aa mind me aad grandfather, an' what he said te me
Of how they fought te get their dues, how unions came te be.

They broke the yearly bond an' the masters' crooked scales.
They fought the blackleg miners from Ireland and Wales.
When torned oot o' their hooses, wey, together they did stand
And they formed the Miners' Union that's known throughout the land.

So we ve got better conditions and better money too,
We've taen the pits unto worselves to see what we can do.
But when we've paid the masters off with interest rates as well,
We'll show them coal's not gannin' back; we'll have a tale te tell.

Wey, with the speeches over, the folks aal torn aroond
Te happins an' te bars an' pubs where fun can now be foond.
There's roondaboots an' shuggy-boats an' dodgem cars se fine,
An' lads an' lasses carryin' on, an' havin' a good time.

Noo, there wes some gannins-on, Aa think they should think shyem,
Aa blushed mesel when Aa went oot inte the back lane.
But then Aa thowt: 'Noo, shut thy gob, thoo's done the same thysel.
For if thoo thowt when thoo was young, thoo'd have a tale te tell.'

Noo, Aa's suppin' beer from dawn till dark, an' mind, Aa had me sup,
For Durham comes but once a year, an' it takes some savin' up.
Although there's fights an' arguments, Aa think we have a right
Te lowse worselves oot once a year, an' end up gettin' tight.

So if ye come wi' me next year, just get your pockets lined.
Fetch the missus an' the bairnies if ye have a mind.
We'll hear the band an' speeches too, an' spend maist o' wor pay,
But we'll have oorsels a bloody good time at the Durham Big Meetin' Day.

Words and music by Johnny Handle

Arthur Scargill on Balcony 1982

photo T. Smith

Kelloe Club, Big Meeting Day

UNITY IS STRENGTH
(with guaranteed gravity)

On my wanderings around the Chester-le-Street area of the County, I came across many retired and some currently employed miners who all seemed to show the same sense of pride in the "Big Meeting" of years gone by and a sense of foreboding about its future. I guess that these feelings will be echoed in communities the length and breadth of Durham and Northumberland; the mainstay of most mining villages being the intangible community spirit and sense of "belonging", born out of mutual dependency.

So to the tale, or anecdote, call it what you will! As in all the best stories it must be shrouded in some mystery, the name of the key player and village, therefore, must remain hidden - to protect the innocent? For the sake of this account, we'll call the village - 'the village', the club shall be known as - 'the Club', and Tommy (oops!) - Tommy is a boisterous man, always game for a bit crack. He enjoys his pint of beer and a game of darts; if he has a fault, it's his blunt manner - you know! the sort who always calls a spade a spade, even when diplomacy and prudence might have called it a shovel. Tommy was not one for bending and it was this argumentative side of him that had caused him to be suffering. At the time of this tale, Tommy was barred from the Club over an argument so trivial in hindsight that it does not rate a mention.

Imagine then the boost to his flagging spirits when he was chosen to carry the banner on Big Meeting Day. Like many a village in County Durham, the day began with parading the Lodge banner through the village. Those men who had been chosen to carry the banner would meet up with the bandsmen at the Club early on Saturday morning and take a couple of pints to put extra spring in their marching and extra gusto into their playing. Thus refreshed, the ritual parade round the village and on the way to Durham City. On such a day as this, surely any small mindedness could be put aside but as the assembled company approached the Club door those thoughts were dashed. "Sorry Tommy - you're barred!" As you might imagine, there were those who pleaded his case but to no avail. Ritual is rarely halted for one man and, besides that, the banner, and the beer, were on the inside so Tommy found himself alone, elbow on knee, sitting on the back step of the Club.

After a while, bandsmen, instruments, poles, ropes and banner all spilled onto the street and Tommy took his place beneath the brightly painted silk and the marching began in earnest.

There were those who remarked during that Big Meeting Day just how well a man of Tommy's temperament had taken the morning's events. Very few, however, saw the open back window at the Club and the row of empty pint glasses standing to attention on the back-step as the band and banner marched away!

Benny Graham (folk-singer)

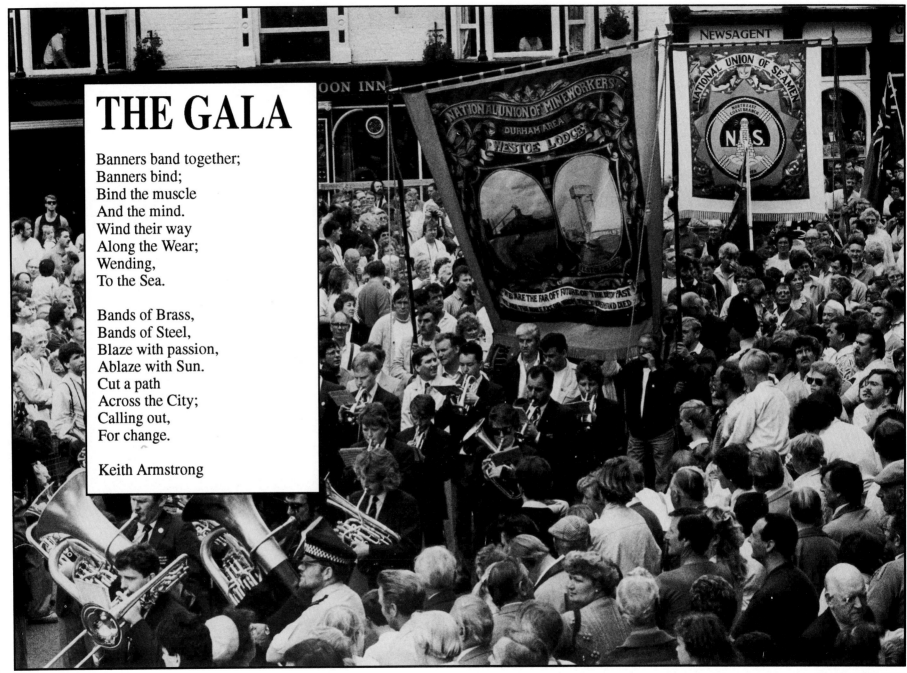

THE GALA

Banners band together;
Banners bind;
Bind the muscle
And the mind.
Wind their way
Along the Wear;
Wending,
To the Sea.

Bands of Brass,
Bands of Steel,
Blaze with passion,
Ablaze with Sun.
Cut a path
Across the City;
Calling out,
For change.

Keith Armstrong

photo Keith Pattison

Big Meeting 1988

Womens Labour Gala 1953   photo Beamish Museum

Racecourse 1950

Bearpark Lodge

BIG MEETING DAYS

We'll never see the like again
when pit-folk to the city came
demanding their reets for a living wage.
This multitude of pioneer
coal-mining pit-folk,
spread a mosaic cloak
marching to bands.
Through the old cobbled streets
their music played,
rallying beneath their great silken picture
slogan banners waved.
Men and boys, side by side,
the light of crusaders battle fire
shining from their eyes.
Over the ancient bridges
to the race course,
this massed throng flowed;
by toil and sweat and blood,
they did not pause,
each heart in union
for this, their sacred cause.
All for one, and one for all,
though dearly wrought, their gospel went,
until, at length, they proved
that 'Unity is Strength.'
Down the years
to the present day,
when the new enlightened generation
of pit-folk
yearly to Durham City make their way,
they have come to renew their faith,
their homage to pay
to those valiant crusaders of the first
Big Meeting Days.

Eve Jobling

FERRY TO THE GALA

I have lived in South Hylton all my life. I am now 83 years old and, having seen your article about the Miners' Gala, I was reminded about the Hylton Colliery. This was a special day.

The miners marched from Castletown, crowds following the band.

The band played all the way down to North Hylton Ferry, everyone trying to keep in step. When they reached the ferry, which was manned by Mr. Ferguson and his son, they only had two rowing-boats. A lot of people had to cross, so the whole process was very slow.

First to cross was the band with all their gear. Now, this was a work of art. The banner, being so big, had to be in just the right position. How they did it, without them all ending up in the river, I'll never know, but, at last, everybody got across, and they all called in to the Golden Lion, which opened up especially for them at 7.30 a.m. They had to catch the 8 o'clock train from South Hylton railway station. The train ran direct to Durham and kept running all day, to cope with all the people.

The band assembled outside the pub, and they marched to the station. Spirits were high and everyone happy. All of South Hylton came to see them off and cheer them on their way.

We were all waiting when they got back, the train returned at 6.00 p.m. They were merry when they went away, and even merrier when they got back! They played at the station for the crowd, they sang and danced then marched again down the Ferry, where the whole thing had to be gone through again. Once across the other side, they had the long walk back to Castletown.

We missed them coming, and it's sad to think there's no more pits around here anymore.

Mrs S. Seymour, (Hylton Bank, Sunderland)

GRESFORD

In Durham's great
Norman Cathedral,
on the coal-miners'
Big Meeting Day,
'GRESFORD',
the anthem of remembrance,
their chosen lodge bands
will play.
And there, at that service,
when they strike up
those first soulful notes,
an awesome mystic magnetism
that anthem's chords evoke,
a stillness most incredible
its mantle enfolds,
cloaking into silence
those gathered Gala folk.
The noise and din of the city,
the racecourse and fairground,
seem to hush,
fade away in that silence,
as those mystic chords abound.
A grave cenotaph quiet
wraps that vast multitude
in union homage
and memories
for their dead uncounted lost.
Thoughts drift
to those coal-seams,
down in earth's
dark dangerous deep,
where day's light
never glows in that blackness,
where sun's rays
never, never will seep;
there, in those hazardous caverns,
where their kin
and their maras sojourn
to win out that coal,
their living to make,
their daily bread to earn
in the ever present danger
to their life, to their limbs,
where fire damp can explode
or the roof come caving in.
Oh, I too well remember
that black gold,
and what it cost them,
for there's blood
on that industry's produce
that gold or time
can never wash away.

And, over that hushed multitude,
this mystic sense profound flows,
till that 'Gresford' lament,
clarion music,
plays its last plaintive notes.
And always some banner
wears that black mourning crepe.
Oh, never, and never, and never
will coal pits be safe.
Aye, today, man must still
make his living
the best way he can,
but God's will
be the judgement
on man's inhumanity
to man.

THE GRESFORD LAMENT.

Eve Jobling, (Ryhope, Sunderland)

WOMEN AND THE GALA

DEVOTED

My father was in Washington Brass Band for 63 years. He played at every Gala and was dedicated to the band. He died on his way back from band practice on a bus. Devoted!

They were up at 7am to set up. And what a family event it was!

You couldn't get on the train platform - packed from before 7am.

If anyone ever said anything against the Gala or the Labour Party they were chucked in the river smartish.

In the miners' strike year there was a very sad atmosphere at the Gala - but we were still proud, even if we were badly done to.

When my father went to his last Gala he dragged his feet. He wasn't well but he was determined - but **he** knew, **we** all knew, it would be his last.

Joan Calvert (Shiney Row)

IT'S OUR DAY!

I remember going to the Gala when I was 11 years old. Mind, it was all families and we were all together, and we'd sit next to our own banners. So you couldn't get lost because you just looked for your banner.

Last year I ended up in tears' because,

you see, we all got on the bus and stopped off at all the OAP homes down the village and the band plays (Easington Band) and my Aunty May lives in one of the homes and they were all out there waiting for us. And the band started to play and me Aunt May started shouting: "It's our day! It's our day! Yi can stand on ya heed if yi like, 'cos it's our day!"

Me mother and her were dancing in the street - and she was shouting.

I was in tears - and one of the Union men saw me and said: "Eeh, your soft as muck under all that toughness aren't yi?"

And we stop off at the Colliery offices and the Pit and the band plays and you look up at that big wheel and you think of all the people who have died in the mines, some of my friends, and the way we were treat like dirt - the pigs, all they have done to us. And all the people around you are thinking the same thing - because you can see it in their faces.

Before the strike, I used to march so determined and proud and we can do this and we can do that; we could beat the world; and now I walk up and its not the same sort of emotion. Yes, I'm still proud but very, very sad of what happened during the strike.

Heather Wood (Easington)

AND THE WOMEN CARRIED THE BANNER

This deputy, George Heatherington was his name, was chairman of the Union and he signed an agreement with the bosses for a reduction in the price of this seam of coal. Of course, the men at the colliery took a dislike to it and they came out on strike because the gaffer wasn't agreeable to give this man his notice. Well the first Pay Friday came round and there was no pay to get. That was when the trouble started. They smashed the blacklegs' windows in. The women got the big drum from the colliery band and were carrying the lodge banner, playing tin-pans, and what have you. Every time the blacklegs rode out of the pit they got paraded down home, but this Pay Friday night, after they did the damage, the police came in a bus-load. They got hold of some men and took them all to Chester-le-Street. Those chaps got 14 days prison and, of course, when they came out of prison, the band was there to meet them, the women carrying the banner and playing the tin-pans and bath-tubs, and they marched away from Chester-le-Street to Fatfield. Just about that time it was Durham Big Meeting and it was the women who carried Cotia banner that day and, of course, it was a great thing because women had never carried the banner into Durham previous to that. I don't know whether they've ever done since, but they did that day. I can mind of some of the women's names. There was Mrs. Ridley and Mrs. Bohill, all big women. The police

daren't have a go at them. That was the idea, they daren't touch the women, but if they'd been men there would have been a bit of a barney. Of course Heatherington had to leave the colliery, that was the only way the men would go back. I wasn't at work at the time, I was at school, but that was the first strike I can remember.

Bill Robson
(from 'Cotia Pit', by G. Purdon)

EVERYTHING IS POLITICAL

My father-in-law loved the Gala so much, he always said "This is our day," "My day", and he really beamed all day. There used to be as many as 15-20 buses leaving Wearmouth for Durham. A family day, tons of people and everyone went.

At one time all the shops and the pubs used to close like as if we were a rabble out to cause trouble. Stupid! there never was much trouble. It was a family day. I'll never

understand that boarding up. Now there are some pubs open and the odd shop but, you know what gets me, the shops have little signs up a week before the Gala: "CLOSED SAT DUE TO DURHAM MINERS' GALA." You feel like an outcast. And they aren't closing so they can let their staff off to have a good time - no, it's a dread to them.

Even though there has been loads of pits closed, there's still a big turn-out every year for the Gala . . . Mind, if you believe what they put in the papers, you would think there was hardly anybody - but you know what they're like - they never print the truth like. 1,000 people when there was 10-15,000. It's ridiculous. It's political, well, everything is political!

Brenda Hopper

THE BANNER RESTS SILENT

The feeling of the Big Meeting Day was like what you get at Christmas - a feeling of goodwill to everyone. And another important thing was the Pit was shut only twice a year - Christmas Day and Big Meeting Day - or at least it was hardly worked, because I can remember the eeriness of the silence at night. We were used to the loud clanking and banging that goes on in and around a Pit. Well, those two days there was silence and I never slept a wink. It was so unnatural.

I don't go to the Gala now. Well, since they closed down Thornley Pit, we all stopped going - the banner rests, silent in the Welfare Hall. It's sad but that's the way it is.

Gladys Bromilow (Thornley)

THE DURHAM WOMEN'S GALA

This area had the most prolific, strongest, women's movement in the country. We used to have a Gala and in 1949 I was chairman of the advisory council for Durham County. I remember the Chief Constable of the County said when we had a Gala in 1949 we had 7,000 in the procession. Nye Bevan and Jenny Lee were the speakers. All sections had banners and we marched through Durham from Old Elvet. All women but we did have men speakers . . . we weren't separatists.

The Durham Women's Gala, I remember that year, it was red hot. we never took our banners to the Miners' Gala. The Miners' Gala was always like a men's do.

I never felt that we were part of the Gala. It was alright with women as long as you didn't rock the boat - stay in the little corner.

I used to load my car up on the Friday night and other people did the same, and we would be on the racecourse 7am Saturday morning and oh it was hard work because the people, oh hundreds and hundreds of people, and, you know, all the food was provided by us women, baking and cooking for days ahead and contributing it for the big day.

Irene McManners (Easington)

GREAT PRIDE

The highlight of that whole day was the Service at Durham Cathedral, waiting for the moment when my grandfather, in a claw hammer coat, came to take up the collection. We all watched with great pride, my grandmother with tears in her eyes, running down her cheeks. We watched him going down the aisle.

"The Gala", they all call it the "Gala", but it was never called that, you know. It was "Big Meeting Day" and, suddenly, someone decided to change its name. I don't like the word "Gala". Some people say "Gayla" some "Gahla", it's daft, like as if it's posh. It was always "The Big Meeting Day", regardless of what they called it.

When my husband Sid died, we held his memorial in the Cathedral and we had a brass band. They didn't play hymns, they played things like "Cushy Butterfield".

Rene Chaplin
(widow of Sid, Durham novelist)

THE GOOD OLD DAYS

The good old days have gone now,
Ne body really wants them back,
But when the ard men get together,
They all start with the crack.

How good it was in the old days,
When you had to struggle for your pay,
The gas, bad stone, and watter,
They loved it; so they say.

"You young lads have seen nothing,"
Will often by their cry,
"If you'd had to hew in two foot nowt,
Why lad, I think you'd die."

They talk with fond affection
Of the Yard and Brockwell seams,
And working in the Harvey,
Three foot of coal - a dream.

They show with pride the big blue scars,
On hands and knees and brow,
Each one worth a hundred pounds,
(That's if they got them now).

Then putting with the gallowas,
In chum out full, don't stop,
And, if they couldn't pull the tubs,
They brayed them with a prop.

Such happy times they recollect,
Of skin scraped off their back,
And overmen who wouldn't pay,
They wish they had them back.

Just to breathe the dust off a big post fault
Or a whiff of the powder reek,
To get out of bed at 2 a.m.
And hear the timber creak.

Paying Banner carriers 1950

Oh the flavour of baccy juice,
Or a nose full of Hedges snuff,
Back shift only once a month
And that was quite enough.

They yearn for jam and bread for bait,
High protein like, you see,
And a bottle of water to wash it down,
None of your pansy tea.

The crack will turn to accidents,
Recalling awful lames,
Of broken legs, and arms pulled out,
And no-one took the blame.

Well, those days are gone, I'm glad to say,

Good riddance to them all,
When men had to work until they dropped,
And got paid bugger all.

So keep your eye on British Coal,
If you work underground,
Cos, if you give them half a chance,
They will try and grind you down.

They'd love to bring the old days back,
When men were nowt but slaves,
So they could stand and crack the whip,
Under the North Sea waves.

Bert Draycott

THE INSIDER LOOKING IN

The 7.30 a.m. band train was the one to be on. There were others going to Durham City, of course, but they were the everyday type where you sat in glum British silence and only looked at your fellow passengers out the corner of your eye.

The band train, however, was packed to capacity with pitmen already fired up with a musical work-out in front of the colliery manager's house and the spine-tingling march to Tyne Dock station.

When a group of people with a common interest get together, there can be something akin to inebriation in the air. A sort of drunkenness without alcohol, a certain loosening of the tongues. And if everyone talked and no one listened, what the hell odds?

This was the Big Meeting, the big day, an all embracing, rumbling, tumbling carnival, of politics, religion, sport, music and beer. Especially beer.

It was the day to meet old acquaintances, make new friends and settle old scores, and not necessarily musical ones at that. It was Derby Day, the Cup Final, Mardi Gras and the Last Night of the Proms all rolled into one.

With bandsmen and officials already shoe-horned into the compartments and corridors of the lumbering, steam train it was common practise to 'stow' newcomers on the luggage racks.

Despite the welter of men and the prospect of a full day's licensed drinking (a rare relaxation of the strict licensing in the early days), the carriages were never vandalised and the train would continue along the coaly litany of stations unmolested. East Boldon, Seaburn, Sunderland, Millfield, Pavillion, Cox Green, Penshaw, Fence Houses and, finally, Durham itself.

With forty or more bands assembling, and upwards of two hundred banners battling the wind, the scene at Durham Railway Station was like the gathering of a medieval army. A hostile medieval army judging by the way the shopkeepers boarded up their doors and windows against the happy mass of people.

In 1951, as Les Telford surveyed the scene for about the fifteenth time, he was once again gripped by the thrill of solidarity shown by the crowds as they packed the narrow streets of the ancient city beneath the disapproving facade of Saint Cuthbert's Cathedral.

This year, however, the crowds were somewhat subdued. True, the black draped lodge banners marking the accidental death of a pitman were a regular feature in the forties and early fifties. With over a hundred pits in the county, it was inevitable that at least one banner would be wearing widow's weaves. And not man-made, non-iron, light weight material. The real stuff, black crepe as thick as Trinidad Lake Asphalt.

In July of that year, the band masters almost to a man preferred solemn music to that of Sousa. Easington Colliery was on everyone's mind.

On the morning of May the twenty-ninth of that year, Les was working on the face in the Harvey seam at Harton Colliery when he was sent for by the foreoverman. Each pit manager was required by law to provide one member of the County Rescue Team for

every two hundred and fifty men employed.

Together with four other members of the Harton Colliery Team, they and their equipment were packed into the pit ambulance and driven to Easington Colliery where in the words of Sam Watson :"A severe explosion had taken place."

The words proved to be something of an understatement for the explosion was one of the most violent ever known before or since. Such was the blast that any item of equipment that projected more than half an inch into the roadway was torn from its moorings: cables, girders, props, kists, telephones, sleepers, conveyor belts - men and ponies.

In the Durham Coalfield, the collieries were roughly divided into two categories, town pits and village pits. In towns like Sunderland, South Shields and Gateshead, they tended to stand aloof from the local community though they were a vital part of the trinity of north-east industry, coal, iron and steel and ship building. In the villages, the pits were invariably the centre of a little universe.

Such was the community spirit in Easington, that the women and children were allowed to use the pit canteen. After forty years it is difficult for us to imagine the mothers taking their children there for a 'treat' in the way we now use Pizza parlours and MacDonalds.

Big Meeting 1991   *photo Stan Gamester*

Easington Memorial 1991   photo Stan Gamester

It was to this community that the Harton Rescue Team arrived on that late, spring morning. Naturally, they were not the first team to arrive for the neighbouring pit teams were already at work. The sight of the anxious crowds, swelling by the minute as relatives from the outlying districts hurried fearfully to the pit, was a sight never to be forgotten.

When the Harton Team were eventually filtered into the relays of men working underground they found that the blast had scoured the main roadway as effectively as a charge of explosive would clear the barrel of a gun.

With their now obsolete liquid oxygen containers strapped to their backs the teams worked slowly but methodically to reach the trapped men. To work too fast might put themselves in danger - indeed two rescuers did die, probably due to the inadequacies of the equipment, but that is another story - too slow and they would not have done justice to any survivors in-bye.

Mine rescue is rather like the procedure for climbing mountains. First organise a headquarters as near to the danger zone as possible, in this case a Fresh Air Base at the shaft bottom, then teams of men to carry equipment closer to the danger area setting in order to set up more bases.

For hours the rescuers sweated, crawled, groped, wordlessly worked their way into the boards and walls. Team after team in six hour relays lugged equipment in-bye. Their breathing apparatus did not allow conversation, perhaps it is just as well, for this was no place for small talk. In the first few hours they found several of their dead colleagues whom they were obliged to bypass in order to concentrate on the search for survivors.

After two days of round-the-clock, unstinting, though fruitless, effort, a decision was made by the officials of the NUM, the NCB and the Mine Rescue Teams that the search would be abandoned.

In their heart of hearts, the rescuers knew this to be the right decision. Despite their efforts, there were no survivors in the district.

Les and his mates were temporarily withdrawn from the pit in order to reorganise the search for bodies and bring the pit back into production.

Two hundred yards of roadway had collapsed due to the iron girders being ripped out and the Rescue Teams laid a light tramway over the top of the fallen stone. The nether strata had 'conveniently' collapsed onto the road leaving a clear passageway over the debris.

A means to ventilate the pit and clear the foul air was required so that the Rescue Teams and volunteers from the Easington work force could go in and bring back their marrers. In all, eighty-five bodies were brought to the surface. Eighty-three Easington men and two rescuers.

The Gala was more than just an excuse for a full day's drinking, it was a time for reflection. In the merciful years, when perhaps only one man was killed in the Durham Coalfield, his family could turn up at the Gala and watch the crowds paying their respects as the black draped banner passed by. A relatively unknown collier perhaps from a remote pit in North West Durham. But the doffing of caps and lowered heads would be a reminder that he was a member of the great brotherhood of coal miners.

After 1951, the Miners' Gala would never be quite the same for Les Telford and the people of Easington.

Ralph Thompson

Big Meeting 1973

THE INSIDER LOOKING OUT

They were taking turns to wash one another's backs. a common ritual in a thousand Pit-head baths.

"Big Meeting on Saturday," commented Dave as he stretched to reach the broad shoulders of the ex-guardsman.

"Aye," said Charlie in a detached sort of way, "Aye."

"Never missed one since . . ." Dave's brow furrowed and he slapped Charlie on the shoulders in annoyance, "You're done. My turn."

"Nineteen forty seven," the large hands worked methodically from shoulders down to waist on the small pitman's blue-scarred back, then, with a flourish. soused the suds away with one great wave of water from his flannel.

"How the hell do you remember when I . . .?

"It was the third anniversary of something that happened on D Day plus thirty . . ."

Dave stepped back into his own cubicle and let the hot spray wash the suds from his bald head, "They're only pitmen you know. Amateurs. Can't expect them to dress up like the Grenadiers." He pointed his lather covered face in Charlie's direction and waited for a reply. When none came he added, "Saw a American marching band there one year. Marching and counter-marching at the double. Seen nowt like it. They were

cheered from the station to the racecourse. You've seen nowt like them Man."

Only the splashing of the water echoed around the baths. Dave raised his face to the spray then shook his head vigorously before switching off the water and reaching for his towel. "It's not all politics, you know."

The big man finished drying his grey hair and began to rub the towel over his shoulders. "There's sex and fighting and drinking. And . . ."

"What's wrong with sex? I met my wife there in, in . . ."

"Nineteen forty seven."

With a huge sigh Dave threw down his towel and padded across the alley to Charlie's shower, "What the hell's the matter with you?" he cried, raising a wet finger at Charlie's chest. "Think you invented morality or summick? Ah wouldn't care. But you're an agnostic."

There was no hostility in the tall man's eyes as he looked down on the bald head and said, "On Monday the sixth of July, nineteen forty seven, you came in the lockers like a dog with two tails."

"Two tails, don't you mean two . . ?" said Dave, who, realising his finger was raised in a hostile manner, pretended to clear his ear of water. "How come you remember the exact bloody date when I can't even . . ."

The tall man was already wrapping the

towel around his waist and padding towards the 'clean' side. Dave followed after him in a welter of warm spray and indignation. "How come. How come you remember 'my' special day?"

They were the only two in the baths and the sweet, fetid smell of the dirty lockers had given way to a tangled aroma of herbal shampoos and scented soap in the 'clean' side. Dave sniffed disapprovingly, "Nowt like this when we were young."

"'Post Operative Battle Trauma' I think they call it now," said Charlie as he pulled on his trousers. "We called it delayed shock. I was going through a bad spell. Third anniversary of . . . When this kid with a mop of hair plastered down with margarine came bounding into the old baths telling anybody who'd listen that he'd 'scored' at the Gala."

Dave's flushed face drooped forward on to his chest. "Aye. well. I remember the deed but not the exact date."

"But did you score?"

"Yes and no. I was born and raised in this colliery. It was "Little Davy Gravy". And, "There goes Titch Marwood". But when I met Mabel I was somebody special."

"So special that she let you . . . The first time you met?"

Dave was wearing flip flops and a towel around his waist when Charlie's accusation hit him. "Right yi big sod. Put up your

THE N.C.B. HAS
CLOSED
OUR COLLIERY
Y?

Hetton Lyons Lodge 1951

photo Keith Pattison

Horden Lodge

mitts." With flaring eyes and bare knuckles, he danced in front of the ex-soldier, totally oblivious to the huge disadvantages in height, weight and reach.

"Come on. Nobody calls my wife and gets away with . . ." He might have went on to a famous victory had not his towel uncoiled to the painted floor.

Charlie looked at Dave's groin and said. "Hit me with that and I'll scream."

For some unknown reason, the colliery baths' supervisor always gave the top lockers to small men and, for once, this worked to Dave's advantage for, after rescuing his towel, he pulled himself onto the metal step and looked Charlie straight in the eye. "Who told you what me and Mabel did on the first day we met?"

"You did," replied Charlie.

Suitably deflated, Dave could only reply, "Aye. Well." Then, after a moment to reflect, added "We all said we did. Even if we didn't. I was only sixteen years . . ."

"I didn't." Charlie hung his soap tray in his locker, took out a comb and began unmatting his hair.

"Nobody thought I had it in me, Chas. First time I'd been with a lass. Had to say summick to impress the lads."

"No you didn't."

For the hundredth time, Dave shook his head. "I don't understand you Charlie. You're the best speaker in the lodge but you won't stand for secretary. You're one of the biggest men in the pit and you won't offer to carry the banner. A teetotaller who signed the petition to get a drinks license in the Institute, a . . ."

"If the lads want to drink then the profits might as well go to the retired members," replied Charlie slamming shut his locker. Then pulling on his cap and squaring his shoulders, he turned to walk away.

"Just a minute YOU big lug. Ah haven't finished yet." Dave tucked his shirt into his trousers and added, "You're the most cantankerous, awkward, contrary, jumped up . . Any chance of a lift to the club?"

The July air enveloped them like a warm fog as they crossed the car park. "Grand day tomorra Charlie. Sure you won't change your mind?"

"What's forty seven from eighty two, Dave?"

"Let's see now. Er, thirty five but what's that got to do with the price of coal."

The big man unlocked his car, "Thirty five years ago tomorrow. Give or take a day or two. You met your Mabel."

For a long time, Dave stood by the passenger door looking at the colliery as though he'd never seen it before. Charlie sat in the driver's seat, took out his glasses, carefully put the case back into his inside pocket, minutely adjusted the rear view mirror, checked the wing mirror then called out to Dave, "Are you ganna stand there all night?"

Like a sleeper awakening, Dave shook his head and got into the car, 'You've shook me Big Un. My oath you have. Thirty five years. Drop me off on the Coast Road will yi?"

"Gonna have one in the Grotto?"

"No. Walk along the cliff tops. Clear me head. You know, when we finally got married, and Mabel came to live here, I started putting on weight. People used to laugh and say she must be a good cook. She was, but the reason I put on weight was because I didn't have to peddle up to Marley Hill colliery three times a week. Three times a week for five years."

The car pulled into the Grotto car park and they sat for a while without talking. Herring gulls and cormorants did slow motion aeronautics in the evening sun over Marsden Rock, and the incoming tide hardly tickled the shore line.

"Wish you'd come Charlie. Just once."

"I've got medals, Dave. Nowt special, campaign medals. Everybody got them, clerks and cooks. Never wear them. I know what I went through over there and don't feel the need to boast about it to others."

As though bidden by gods, they got silently out of the car and walked hands deep in trouser pockets to the cliff edge. Far to the north, Saint Mary's lighthouse glowed in the late evening sun.

"It's the fellowship Charlie. And the way people talk to men from other collieries, as though they'd known them all their lives. Oh, I know they're not the same as your army mates, but . . ."

"No, they're not, Dave. They're better."

"Better? I thought, well, all that shot and shell would . . ."

"Forge closer links?"

A herring gull screamed overhead.

"Aye. Closer links."

"No. If ever I was in danger, real danger. I'd sooner be in it with pitmen than any other group of men. Can't explain why. Just something inside. Anyway, I don't have to explain it. Same as I don't have to wear my medals to prove where I was on D Day plus thirty. It's all here inside." He tapped his forehead.

For a long time they stood on the cliff edge looking out to sea. Dave took out a packet of fags and automatically offered one to Charlie who shook his head. "You know I don't smoke Marra."

"Sorry Mate. I was miles away. Remember that book you lent me?"

"What book."

"The only one you ever lent me. About the pitmen?"

"Oh. The Sid Chaplin one?"

"Aye. That one."

"What about it?"

Dave took a long drag on the fag. "He said we're all Cuddie's people. The good, the-not-so-good and the bad. Don't you see? We're all marras in Saint Cuthbert's eyes. Oh, I forget, you're an agnostic."

For once, the big man looked ruffled. "Aye, but I'm still one of Cuddie's people. One of the great brotherhood of pitmen . . ."

"Prove it."

"I don't have ti."

"You went to the Cenotaph one Remembrance Sunday."

"Aye. Well that was . . ."

"To celebrate the the passing of men who died on foreign fields?"

"Aye."

"Well, what about the men, women and boys who perished under English fields?"

The big man turned away and looked towards Shields' piers where a mail boat was about to leave. He watched as it slid silently passed the Collingwood Memorial and the ruins of Tynemouth Priory.

"Come on Big Un. What about it?"

"Alright then. But just this once. And remember. No smoking in my car. And no drinking, fighting or chasing women when we get there."

"You're on Mate." Dave shook the big man's hand. "No fighting or chasing women. Pick me up at nine o'clock tomorra. Tara. Think I will have one in the Grotto after all." He turned and hurried towards the steps that led down to the beach.

"Just a minute Dave," Charlie called out to the hurrying figure. "You said, 'No fighting or chasing women.' What about the . . ."

The little pitman was half way down the first flight of stairs when he shouted out over his shoulder, "We're all Cuddie's people. The good and the bad. Just put me down as a not-so-good."

Ralph Thompson

NOT QUITE ON THE INSIDE

I remember how small he looked when we laid him to rest. Yet, when he was younger, I could have sworn he was at least ten feet tall. Especially when he was wearing his bandsman's uniform. Yes, memories do deceive, yet a lump still comes to my throat when I hear a brass band.

With his gold braid and shiny buttons, I used to imagine that he ought to have stood on the balcony of Buckingham Palace, for he was far more handsome than Edward the Eighth.

Not to be outdone in the dress department, my mother and I carefully prepared our outfits. No casual wear for Missus Craske and daughter. Like everyone else, we wore our Sunday best - whatever the weather.

When I was a girl there were three important events each year; Christmas, my birthday, and Durham Gala Day.

Gala Day was planned more meticulously than Christmas, for no sooner would the banners be put away, than preparations for next year's Meeting would begin. At Whitburn Colliery, for instance, where my dad worked, the union would dock money off the wages each week in order to pay for the family's train tickets.

Although this was a family occasion, it took me years to realise that for ours it was a

photo Newcastle Chronicle   *Big Meeting 1958*

strangely divided day. Mam and Dad would be up early, Mam pressing the creases into the immaculate trousers, and Dad polishing his boots and buttons.

By the time I awoke, Dad would be resplendent and standing by the range waiting for his good luck kisses, for he would leave early to catch the band train. Then the important business would begin. What to wear?

We invariably dressed in hats, gloves and coats, regardless of the temperature. Dressing up was half the fun, the other half

involved dressing down our rivals in the fashion stakes. "Far too old for that hemline." "That hat's seen more Galas than the County Hotel." "I see the fox fur's come out of the pawn shop for its early outing."

Goodness knows what was said about us, but what odds? We didn't have wall-to-wall Soap Operas to talk about and, anyway, it's always better to gossip about someone you knew.

The high point of the day would come

after what seemed an endless train journey and much tramping about in fashionable, though not necessarily comfortable, shoes. Dad was something of a musical mercenary and might play for a different band each year.

We'd stand on the pavement craning our necks, until the particular banner blustered into view. What a sight, what a feeling! A family united in one resplendent, musical moment. A fusion of sound, colour and tears.

After the parade and the speeches and the picnic tea, I'd be taken to the fair, another never-to-be-forgotten-once a year-spectacular. Then the row would start.

Dad would always insist on going back to the colliery whose band he'd played in. "To receive the accolades of the residents of that village who hadn't made it to the Gala." A likely story. The long summer day would draw to a close before he staggered homeward.

So that was it. A day that had everything. Colour, excitement, music, tears of joy, a family row, crowds, tears of sorrow.

As each colourless year passes, the more I'd give for one hour to be spent on the streets of Durham City waiting for the band to come.

Ralph Thompson
(based on a local woman's story)

64

Jack Charlton 1980

LIST OF GALA DATES AND SPEAKERS 1958 - 1983

75. 1958, July 19th.—The Rt. Hon. J. H. Wilson, M.P.; The Rt. Hon. A. Robens, M.P.; Miss Alice Bacon, M.P.; A. L. Horner, Esq., Secretary, National Union of Mineworkers.

76. 1959, July 18th.—The Rt. Hon. A. Bevan, M.P.; C. P. Mayhew, M.P.; A. Blenkinsop, M.P.; W. Paynter, Esq., Secretary, National Union of Mineworkers.

77. 1960, July 16th.—F. E. Noel-Baker, M.P.: F. T. Willey, M.P.; C. F. Grey, M.P.; W. Paynter, Esq., Secretary, National Union of Mineworkers.

78. 1961, July 15th.—The Rt. Hon. H. T. N. Gaitskell. M.P.; Mrs. Bessie Braddock, M.P.; Michael Foot, M.P.; W Paynter, Esq., Secretary, National Union of Mineworkers.

79. 1962, July 21st.—Mr. Anthony Wedgwood Benn; The Rt. Hon G. A. Brown, M.P.; Mrs. B. A. Castle, M.P.; W. Paynter, Esq., Secretary, National Union of Mineworkers.

80. 1963, July 20th.—Rt. Hon. J. H. Wilson, M.P.; Mr. L. J. Callaghan M.P.; Mr. M. M. Foot, M.P.; W. Paynter, Esq., Secretary, National Union of Mineworkers.

81. 1964, July 18th.—Rt. Hon. G. A. Brown, M.P.; Mr. A. Wedgwood Benn, M.P.; Frank Cousins, Esq.; W. Paynter. Esq., Secretary, National Union of Mineworkers.

82. 1965. July 17th.—Rt. Hon. L. J. Callaghan, M.P., Chancellor of the Exchequer; Rt. Hon. G. A. Brown. M.P.; (Rt. Hon. R. J. Gunter, M.P., Minister of Labour, unable to attend); Mr. M. Foot, M.P.; W. Paynter. Esq., Secretary, National Union of Mineworkers.

83. 1966. July 16th.—Rt. Hon G. A. Brown. M.P., Deputy Prime Minister; (Rt. Hon. J. H. Wilson, O.B.E., M.P., Prime Minister. unable to attend); Rt. Hon. A. Wedgwood Benn, M.P., Postmaster General; Rt. Hon. M. M. Stewart, M.P., Foreign Secretary; W. Paynter, Esq., Secretary, National Union of Mineworkers.

84. 1967. July 15th.—Rt. Hon. L. J. Callaghan, M.P., Chancellor of the Exchequer; Rt. Hon. R. J. Gunter, M.P., Minister of Labour; Mr. M. Foot. M.P.; W. Paynter, Esq., Secretary. National Union of Mineworkers.

85. 1968, July 20th.—Rt, Hon. Mrs. Barbara Castle, M.P., Secretary of State for Employment and Productivity; Rt. Hon. Richard Marsh, M.P., Minister of Transport; Rt. Hon. A. Wedgwood Benn, M.P., Minister of Technology; W. Paynter, Esq., Secretary, National Union of Mineworkers.

86. 1969, July 19th.—Rt. Hon. Roy Mason, M.P., Minister of Power; Michael Foot, M.P.; Rt. Hon. Judith Hart, M.P., Paymaster General; L. Daly, Esq., Secretary, National Union of Mineworkers.

87. 1970, July 18th.—Rt. Hon. Mrs. Barbara Castle, M.P.; Rt. Hon. A. N. Wedgwood Benn, M.P.; L. Daly, Esq., Secretary, National Union of Mineworkers. (Sir Sidney Ford ill).

88. 1971, July 17th.—Vic. Feather, C.B.E.; The Right Rev. T. T. Ramsey, D.D. (Lord Bishop of Durham).; Baroness Lee of Asheridge.

89. 1972, July 15th.—Michael Foot, M.P.; Rt. Hon. A. Wedgwood Benn, M.P., Joe Gormley, Esq., President, National Union of Mineworkers

90. 1973, July 21st.—Rt. Hon. J. H. Wilson, M.P.; W. W. Hamilton, M.P., L. Daly, Esq., Secretary, National Union of Mineworkers.

91. 1974, July 20th.—Rt. Hon. A. Wedgwood Benn, M.P.; Rt. Hon. Michael Foot, M.P.; Joe Gormley, Esq., President, N.U.M.

92. 1975, July 19th.—Rt. Hon. L. J. Callaghan, M.P.; L. Daly, Esq., Secretary, N.U.M., Rt. Hon. Shirley Williams. M.P.

93. 1976, July 17th.—Rt. Hon. Michael Foot, M.P.; Rt. Hon. A. Wedgwood Benn, M.P.; L. Daly, Esq., Secretary, N.U.M.

94. 1977, July 16th.—E. S. Heffer, M.P.; Arthur Scargill; L. Daly, Esq., Secretary, N.U.M.

95. 1978, July 15th.—Rt. Hon. A. Wedgwood Benn, M.P.; D. Skinner, M.P.; L. Daly, Esq., Secretary, N.U.M.

96. 1979, July 21st.—Rt. Hon. Michael Foot, M.P.; Jimmy Reid; Joe Gormley, Esq., President, N.U.M.

97. 1980, July 12th.—Rt. Hon. A. Wedgwood Benn, M.P.; Arthur Scargill; Joe Gormley, Esq., President, N.U.M.

98. 1981, July 11th.—Neil G. Kinnock, M.P.; Emlyn Williams; L. Daly, Esq., Secretary, N.U.M.

99. 1982, July 10th.—D. Skinner, M.P.; E. Clarke; Arthur Scargill, Esq., President, N.U.M.

100.1983, July 16th.—N. G. Kinnock, M.P.; A. N. Wedgwood Benn, M.P., L. Daly, Esq., Secretary, N.U.M.

photo Newcastle Chronicle

Big Meeting 1975

Woodland Colliery Lodge

photo Beamish Museum

IN THEM DAYS:

Memories of the Miners' Gala

(extracts from the booklet published by Gilesgate Junior School to commemorate the Gala Centenary in 1983)

TRAVELLING IN

The people marched from the village into Durham to claim their rights, the right to work and to earn money; they drew lots to see who was going to carry the banner. At the top of the village, the men would gather with the brass band, and they would march from the top of the village right through, and they would stop at various points and wave to people, from one end of the village to the other. And then they would get into one of these old buses and drive off to Durham. It was the same in every village; they would meet, usually the Working Men's Club, and everything would be ready. And often they would have a drink and a dance the night before. Many of them would be gathering at half-past five, getting the banner out, getting the band ready, and I could hear this as a child, you see. You knew when it was Miners' Gala Day, because, on that morning, as you were lying in bed, suddenly you would hear the sound of a band in the distance, building up, and the noise of a band as it passed your window, and you could look out and see all the bright uniforms. The band we had had bright red uniforms and black trousers, and looked very smart, with

Big Meeting 1964

the big banner, and everybody waving and cheering. It was really a holiday, a big holiday.

TRAVELLING OUT AGAIN!

Twelve hours non-stop drinking. Durham was packed. It just went on all night. It was nothing to walk along the racecourse on a Sunday morning and see thirty or forty people asleep on the grass, been there all night, just hadn't got home. And, of course, before the thirties, there wasn't the transport to get them home.

"THAT'S WHAT IT'S ALL ABOUT"

You really could feel the solidarity of Socialism on that day. You could feel it in the air; it was sort of like walking in a fog. Everybody was sort of comrades. Even if you were small, you knew it was something very special. You'd watch people walking under the banners and they'd been working for maybe forty years, and when you've worked hard for that long it shows on your face. And they were very proud, marching under the banners. It was every miner's wish to be drawn to carry the banner. There's great solidarity between the miners, perhaps more than between any other group of blue

Racecourse 1950

collar workers, because, when you were underground like, everybody was dependent on everybody else, and, if anything goes wrong down there these lads will dig at the earth with their finger nails to get their pals out. There's terrific solidarity down there. Mind you, when you come to bank (to the surface), sometimes it doesn't seem to be there so much as when you're going in-Bye (going down into the pit). But when you had the Big Meeting then they all seemed to come together again, and with the power of the bands and the music and the feeling in the air, you can really feel it. Everybody used to shout across the road to people they worked with, even if you'd only seen them the day before.

IN THE WATER

There are several garbled versions of this famous story. In fact, Bishop Henson was unpopular with the miners, but it was the Dean of Durham, Dean Welldon, who was jostled by the miners and his umbrella and hat which were thrown into the river on July 25, 1925. One of the banners that year read: "To Hell with Bishops and Deans! We want a living wage."

One year the bishop had been saying something bad about the miners . . . and another bishop came down onto the racecourse, and the miners got a bit vexed about it when they saw the bishop was come, so they got hold of the wrong bishop, and tried to throw him in the river. But, just in time, Mr. Brown, who owned the boathouse, came along with his boat and managed to rescue him, and he got away before they did any damage.

HAPPY DAYS

It was very very rare for it to rain in them days. Mind, now, the weather's changed, but it used to be sweltering. They came in their uniforms, but going back out they were in shirt-sleeves and all that, you know, no coats on, and there they were, just rolling about with the banners. You'd think to yourself, eee! no, he cannot carry that banner, but, by gum, he does, and the fellow at the back with his string, and they were absolutely sozzled. But you never saw any violence in them days. They were happy, tight as they were, dancing and singing. Some were all dressed up in costumes, not for a competition or anything, but for fun.

When I was just a bairn, we used all to walk in with the banner from Sherburn, from Sherburn Hill. They always used to have a draw among the miners for who would carry the banner in and who would carry it out. I remember, and I wasn't very old, and my father drew it; his name got drawn out to carry it out of Durham. Now anybody could carry a banner in, but when y're carrying a banner out . . . people had been boozing, which in them days they did do, they boozed all the time, and I've never forgotten my poor father, they had to help him . . . people had to help him to carry it. It wasn't my father, he didn't drink, but they were all tugging on it you know.

When they marched the banner, it was carried, one on either side; there was a big man carried the pole. And, like the soldiers do for carrying the standard, they had a strap round their neck with a little tub at the bottom for the rest of the pole of the banner, and you carried that with your arms up so it must have very very tiring. They marched miles doing that. At either side of each pole, there was a cord with a tassle on it, and

there were four people who held on, so that there was one person at each string. And the lodge officials walked right underneath the banner, with their little case with the money in to pay the men, and they paid the banner carriers who got a consideration for carrying it. I've seen the banner folded up to go out because they couldn't carry it, 'cos they were so drunk. The bands played any old thing coming out; I mean they didn't just play one tune, they played two or three different tunes.

More often that not, they had to roll them up and carry them home. The people holding the banners had two or three people holding them up often. They was all right coming in but coming home it was a different story.

All the banners are coming up the streets, and it's good, but when they're going out, two men are holding the banner, and two men at that side are holding the cords, and two men at this side too, to keep it straight. Now that's all right going in, but, coming out, they're drunk; they've just had a good day and they're drunk. So the banners is going this way, and they're going that way, and it's great!

They'd draw the names out of a hat for who was going to carry the banner, and there were two bannermen, one on each pole and four men on the ropes to control the top of the banner. You can imagine, if the polemen were drunk, and the string-men were drunk, everybody used to be helping them. It was a very funny sight. It used to be going forwards and backwards and sideways all over.

RIVER FUN

On the river, all the boats were hired out, and they were falling into the river, some of them that had too much to drink, you know, and carrying on, and they were rolling out of the boat into the river. Lads used to jump from the Bridge for a dare, all good suits on they used to jump in. Then the police stopped them because it's very dangerous; it gets very shallow there and there are rocks on the bottom. But they always used to have boat fights, deliberate; the lads used to hire those punts, and there'd be two or three of them in each punt, and they'd come over with the pole and use that to push the others out of the boat, like the knights used to joust, using the pole like a lance, but there were no points on; and everybody by the riverside used to stand there and watch the lads doing that; it was a big laugh when they all went in.

CLEANING UP

When I was young, about sixteen, we lived in the middle of Gilesgate Bank, and we had a house with quite a big windowsill and quite a deep step. And we always collected up the glasses because they used to dump them. They'd mebbies sit on your step and leave the glass. And the publicans on a Sunday morning would come round and collect up all their belongings.

On Sundays, what a sight! And it used to take ten women a week to clean up on the racecourse. They do it yet. They used to put strings down and they had to pick up the broken glass and things up in strips; they had to comb the grass, you know.

There used to be loads of drunks lying around, blokes all over the grass and that, and, of course, us kids loved that; we wouldn't roll them in those days; we weren't muggers, but when they used to sober up and get up and go away there used to be always two bobs and half-crowns and things lying all over that just used to roll out their pockets, you see, and they were so drunk they just didn't realise what they were losing. You used to be able to go down on a Sunday morning, and we did literally used to clean up pounds and pounds lying around on the grass.

And on a Sunday morning you could look out of the window, and see blokes lying all over the place that hadn't been in the land of the living to get the bus, drunk as noodles. They were out for the count.

South African Miners address 1992 Big Meeting

PUBS, POLITICS, AND PUNCH-UPS

The first time I went to Durham Big Meeting was in 1961, when I was 16 years old. Although my father had been a pitman in Blackhall for a few years, I was brought up in Hartlepool. We traditionally regarded people from the collieries as 'coalybacks', 'yakkers', or 'underground savages'. I was quite surprised upon meeting a few, to find they were really quite civilised and amazingly friendly.

I had heard stories about the Big Meeting, but nothing prepared me for the reality. I caught the bus to Durham with a few teenage friends, and we could get no closer than the New Inn. The streets were crammed with people - I was told that on that day there were over 100,000 people in the city - but we managed to make our way to stand outside the County Hotel. Being quite small, I could see very little of the actual marchers,

so what sticks in my mind is the sight of the most beautiful banners going past. There were pictures of Marx and Engels, Kier Hardie, Arthur Cook, and more local heroes such as Peter Lee. And the slogans. 'Unity is Strength', 'The Cause of Labour is the Hope of the World'. It was very exciting and moving for a teenager just getting involved in politics.

We followed the crowd to the Racecourse for the speeches. I remember that Bessie Braddock was one of the speakers. Being young firebrands, we gave her a bit of good-natured heckling. The response was amazing. She almost foamed at the mouth, and accused us of taking 'Moscow Gold' (being paid by the communists). Between the four of us we had maybe fifteen shilling in our pockets. In subsequent years, I saw all the Labour leaders apart from Callaghan, but what was more moving was seeing speakers from South Africa, Chile, Vietnam talking about the real life or death struggles of their people for freedom.

Bill Broome

photo Keith Pattison

Horden Banner 1980s

photo Newcastle Chronicle

Marching onto Racecourse

WAITING FOR A BANNER: 1982

Mount Pleasant Bank was sparsely lined,
Few had left an open door
To lean upon a gate and wait . . .
For the banner coming back.
Old hands cracking in afternoon sun;
Clutching, bewildered hands,
Directing gaze, anticipating,
Memories marching.
No middle years, just empty space
The treadmill of illusion long since
Took their 'Big Meeting' place
And tears of the politic eye
Splash quiet on the new hearts . . .
Rain kissing glass.

We waited, refugees from a forgotten state
And children from a new one,
Breathing new air on old ways
And old air uncomfortably.
Bridging years guiltlessly
With understanding looks.
That knowledge words can never build.

I waited impatient for the euphony
Of brass to prick my ears.
Orphaned from long gone Gala days
Of riding strong shoulders,
Work stretched, blue scarred,
Loss filmed my eyes
Though I had lost no-one.
The chrysalis of memory stirred in sleep.
Banners going home . . .

Keir Hardy, Nye Bevan, all the woven
heroes,
Silk wove on a silk worm.
Angels reaching out to desperate hands,
Hell on blackened faces
Appealing to serenity, unfurled,
Above bobbing heads of many alas gone.

The Pleasant crest was lit
by a flame between two spears,
Kicking shameless at the wind;
UNITY IS STRENGTH
Every crimson curling inch a revolution,
Blood in ballet on the breeze.
No less a returning conqueress
For time weaned army
Or hackneyed hymn.

A. Cutting

LOOKING BACK

Clear water drips onto once shining rails,
Filtered through strata gleaned from the dales,
The labyrinths are silent, void of men's voices,
No laughter, cries, or the crudest of curses.

Between distorted ring-girders, stone buries the past,
Claiming back ground from the shotfirers' blast,
The faces close to meet the floor,
Crushing stout timbers, put there decades before.

There is no trace of the blood that's been spilled,
No evidence left of the men who've been killed.
Even the rats have deserted this intricate maze,
Littered with broken, rusting, equipment that's seen better days.

Young timber-lads' graffiti adorn the rock slab,
The deputy they wrote about is now old and sad.
No more a threat with shouted, stern, orders,
Most of his underlings are now grandfathers.

There must still be somewhere a broken flask,
The one I left behind all those years past.
I was crawling off the face in a hurry to get home,
It broke in my pocket, I threw it in the goaf.

I wonder where they put my boots when they cut them off,
And my kneepads too with the broken straps.
Or the old cowboy belt that held my battery,
Lying rotting, no doubt, in the pitch black galleries.

Under the blackened chimneys of the little colliery houses,
Was more life than in any of Shakespeare's dramas.
I've been honoured to be born amongst God's children,
In a world awash with laughter, love and compassion.

Ron Gray

DURHAM MINERS' GALA

Dig deep. Dig deep
To the heart of this Durham day.
Beyond the obvious pageant
As bands blast on their way.
Let not the cries of other years
Be drowned by your wild drums
Or be lost in the swirl of greetings
For each proud banner that comes.

Think on. Think on
This is the sunny end.
Know that these men's forefathers
Had no Union for a friend.
In days when they needed pity
No pity could ever be found
For starved and hounded pitmen,
Lost slaves in the underground.

Big Meeting 1930s

photo Beamish Museum

To speak. To speak
For justice no man dared;
Coal-owners owned men's bodies
In a land where no one cared.
Remember the miners' children
Destroyed in the lust for coal
Through deep dark hours that clouded
The morning of their soul.

Go back. Go back.
Turn a century's page
Read in lines that run with blood
How they lived in a merciless age.
How they tried to stand together
But were crushed by lords of the land.
Learn of families that lived in fields
Who made the first valiant stand.

Recall. Recall
As you march by the County Hotel,
The sacrifice of men who made
Your first step out of hell.
Dance in the sun of Old Elvet
Though ghosts in the shadows weep.
Remember the light in your darkness;
The first voice out of the deep.

Bob Davison

HIS BRIGHT SILVER

SONG (traditional)

The bonny pit laddie
The canny pit laddie
The bonny pit laddie for me O

He sits on his cracket
And hews in his jacket
And brings the bright siller to me O

1.

Pit-yackers dance to
Pully-wheel buzzer

At Kelloe the calf hill
Chipped cross-face of Helen

At Hetton and Elemore
Trimdon and Esh

Little Chance is the gallowa
Putters all bless

2.

Beech candles drip wax
Into root-fibre cutting

Full draped bier
Draws empty one up

On twisted steel rope
On gravity bobbins

As children whirl haloes
Discarded hemp-core lit

3.

Stephenson's steam theodolite
Spies lay for waggon line

Lambton Hetton and Joicey's logo
Bold on wooden sides

Wheel-squeak and larks
Sing along with fossil birds

Embanked through bowed reapers
Eden's last harvest falls

4.

Brick warren estate
Rabbit Wood overrun

High rise shadow-blade
Has steel cord cut

Ghostly crossing keeper
Muffler clay pipe and spit

Old 'face' now 'bank man'
Like Hefaenricaes Uard
Dreams and puffs his twist

5.

Hazeldene evensong
Church on green edge

Sunset banner
Starboard tapers lit

Deep bramble harrowing
Chancel-bow dip by Gox

Pit-head Malkuth
In bent barley

6.

Memorial words
Uncial Quarter seam

Bonny May morning
Night shift on the face

Telltale yellow cage bird
First shift in the Gate poor lads

Black explosion banner
Stone names all but one

7.

Candles flicker in eviction tents
What Kingdom without common feasting

When they were seated
Silk banners on fellside

Friends after nettle broth
Turned slogans into bread

By the poor for the poor
They taught themselves

8.

Street children cry Cockerooso
Generations hop across

Spuggie chorus crack
Cathedral choir sing anthem

"Our feet shall stand
In thy gates O Jerusalem"

Larks rise with brass
Big Meeting last one for Eden

9.

The bonny pit laddie
Sits on his cracket

Corf fill the Keel
Keel fill the brig

Dark drift or shaft hole
He hews in his jacket

And brings the bright silver
The canny pit laddie

His eye full of silver to me

William Martin

photo T. Smith

photo Beamish Museum

Grim faces at Big Meeting in 30s

Harold and Mary Wilson on Balcony

TONY BENN'S GALA MEMORIES

(interviewed at The House of Commons by Keith Armstrong and Dave Gaston)

The first Gala I spoke at was in 1962, then every other year since, though they let me off one year so that I could attend the Centenary Gala. I think it's more than anybody else, about sixteen times.

I particularly remember the Gala in 1980 when there were four speakers - Jim Callaghan and Joe Gormley, Arthur Scargill and myself. It was like the men's doubles at Wimbledon. Because Arthur warned of pit-closures and I had just been Secretary of State for Energy, and Gormley pooh-poohed the idea that the Government would attack the pits. That was one I remember.

All the meetings depended so much on what the mood was. I mean in 1974, just after we'd got in, it was tremendous, yet in 1980 we were a bit down.

Sometimes you were trying to catch the mood of optimism and push it forward, sometimes you were trying to check the mood of pessimism.

It is without any doubt the most remarkable occasion though, of course, the number of pits, when I first went, was 120.

The first time I went, Sam Watson was the General Secretary. I remember, after the dinner at the County Hotel, Sam Watson got up and made a little speech. He said "All the women serving the meal are miners' daughters and one of them has just been admitted to a place at University", and George Brown

shouted "Shame!" I thought that was one of the most significant events.

In 1966, at the dinner beforehand, George Brown told me he was going to resign from the Government and he confirmed it on the Balcony the following morning - Harold Wilson had gone to Moscow and it was just before what were called 'the July Measures' which destroyed the National Plan.

I remember unveiling the banner at Horden Lodge and I used to go every year with Bearpark Lodge and stop at the 'Dog and Gun'.

Sam Watson

A younger Tony Benn

I also remember participating in a celebration at Tommy Hepburn's grave, and I put Tommy Hepburn onto a postage stamp, there was a hell of a row about that!

I think the Gala ought to be a major national day, a sort of May Day, particularly if the Government abolish the holiday.

I've always found it very, very moving indeed. The other thing is that you're voted to speak by the Lodges, you're not picked by the General Secretary and his friends or whatever.

The Chief Constable used to come to the dinner beforehand and sing a song and then you had the Lord Mayor and the rest. I always felt I was going to the Execution Block when you marched with those guys!

Sam Watson always used to boast that "it

was the biggest unorganised demonstration in the world," because people turned up and the Lodges sorted things out their own way.

It always gave me pleasure to be told that on one occasion they threw the Bishop into the river!

I had a flaming row with Sam Watson the first time I was invited to the Gala. He wrote to me at the time of my Peerage case when I'd just been thrown out of Parliament. His letter went 'Dear Lord Stansgate, the miners have voted you to speak at the Gala'. So I wrote back 'Dear Sam, I'm very honoured but if I came I couldn't possibly be described as "Lord Stansgate".' So Sam wrote back and said that 'your name appears on the Ballot that way and I'm not prepared to have you here under any other circumstances.' My reply was that 'I'm engaged in a huge constitutional struggle and I cannot compromise it by appearing in that way.' I thought that was the end of it but, in the end, what they did was to put in the programme 'Benn', and then, underneath in brackets, 'Lord Stansgate'.

It sounded so bureaucratic I couldn't believe it! Apparently the reason was that one year they'd put the wrong name on the ballot and invited Francis Noel-Baker, who was an absolute rogue and the son of Phillip Noel-Baker, who'd won a Nobel Peace Prize. Because they'd put the wrong name on the ballot, they had to have Francis when they'd really wanted Phil. So they always had to have the person whose name was on the ballot.

Gormley 1980

you scratch a shop-steward in Bristol, you've got a lay-preacher; if you scratch a shop-steward, or a branch official, in Geordieland, you've got an ex-Sergeant from the Grenadier Guards. This sense of loyalty I find an amazing characteristic of Geordies.

The Tories are destroying the Mining Industry, destroying local communities, then they strip them with the open-cast and destroy the local environment as well,

Sam was a terrible old disciplinarian, a remarkable man, very upright, but about as right wing as you could find anywhere in the Labour Party, a Gaitskellite and so on.

I remember one colliery band stopping and turning towards the platform and Harold Wilson was there. It was a colliery which had been closed that year by a Labour Government and the song they played was 'Congratulations', and Harold said to me "Do you hear that!" It was such a strange thing, they'd obviously picked the song before the announcement of closure!

If you scratch a shop-steward on Clydeside, you've got a Marxist agitator; if

photo Stan Gamester *Big Meeting 1992*

importing coal from South Africa and Colombia where the working conditions are appalling. And we've got 1,000 years of coal under our territory and the world reserves of coal four times as great as of oil and nuclear power is three times as expensive. To destroy that industry is probably the greatest act of betrayal of what you might call 'the national interest' as there has every been and then, of course, you wait and see, when they privatise it, they'll have all those ads about British Coal being more productive then ever so they can sell the damned stuff off.

Nye Bevan 1950

Big Meeting 1975

photo Newcastle Chronicle

DENNIS SKINNER'S GALA MEMORIES

(interviewed at The House of Commons by Keith Armstrong and Dave Gaston)

I think the first time I went was in '78 when Callaghan was Prime Minister. Because you're not allowed to speak in consecutive Galas, speakers are voted in every two years and I've been voted in every two years since '78, with the exception of the Miners, Strike when I was asked to speak out of turn - there were three years in succession at that point.

I never thought in my wildest dreams, when I was a young man working in the pits before I came to Parliament, that I would have been stood on a platform at the Durham Miners' Gala which I knew all about. Because I wasn't a national speaker.

The first time I spoke at Durham was awesome, much more so than coming to Parliament. To be on that platform to me

Dennis Skinner addressing Big Meeting 1992

Listening to Dennis Skinner, Big Meeting 1992

was more of a tribute and more important to me than walking through those doors. I can't remember coming through those doors but I can remember being at my first Durham Miners' Gala and on the Balcony at the County Hotel.

I make an effort with every speech at the Gala. I don't want to kid you on. When I speak, a lot of the people think it's totally

Wearmouth Miners 1984/1985 Strike   photo Keith Pattison

extempore but I do think very seriously about what I'm going to say. I think the most memorable one, without a doubt, was the strike year when the dockers were out and I can still remember standing on the platform and saying "The Sun is out, the miners are out and now the dockers are out," and I could have returned to my seat then. I've always tried to inject humour into my speeches, not humour for humour's sake, but political and industrial humour that is, in a way, satire. You make a mess of it in here because it's a small audience but it always works at a big rally. If you are tilting at windmills in a political and industrial fash-

ion, you've got to have a mixture of those who will respond to the crude and banal and those who will seize on the more sophisticated point and I've enjoyed every minute of it.

I think the Gala has managed to get through that period when there was an attempt to shove it on one side. The Beamish thing was an attempt, without doubt to sideline it, but it didn't work. I don't think it will diminish seriously from the present position. I find, more and more, that there are people coming from other parts of Britain to attend the Gala, just like

they go to the Chesterfield May Day Rally.

I don't think we're going to let it die. Even though you're not going to get the 200 odd thousand I suppose were there when there was 150 pits, it will continue; I've no doubt at all about that. Lots of people will clamour to be able to speak there - everyone I know that gets on that platform feels ten feet tall, it's still the one where people like to think they've made it. The Durham Gala is the No. 1.

I can also remember a lot of them leaving when Kinnock got up and didn't give total, wholehearted, support to the Strike. I've still got the imagery of those groups with the bands and the banners marching back up in the distance, away up the path. I've still got that picture in my mind.

To me that was an incredible period, because it looked as if we had a chance. It was one of the few occasions during the 1984-1985 Strike on that Saturday morning, when it was possible to say, because I never told lies in the Strike, I never kidded people on that it was a cake-walk - but that morning, in my bones, I knew that there was just half a chance, if the dockers could keep out for any period of time, and with the deputies getting restless. It was a morning when my hopes were high and it was reflected in a lot of the people that I met there, there was a confident and jaunty feeling, there were possibilities no doubt. But then, of course, they didn't get the Felixstowe people out and they didn't get the Dover people out. What the T&G should have done was put up for a big wage claim of 20% or whatever and frightened the bosses to death and I think

then that Dover and Felixstowe would have come out. None of the other unions saw the need to join the Strike by putting in for a big wage-claim. The railwaymen did it at the beginning, but the Government picked them off and paid them that bit extra because they didn't want a second front.

The TUC's role was one of retreat and failure to respond, they just pussy-footed. They should have co-ordinated actively, they should have been in there, got rid of the Tory Government and changed the history of the Movement. Big changes always take place outside of this place anyway. The Miners' Strike provided the opportunity for a shift in that patchwork quilt that's repre-

sented by the bosses. We could have knocked a bloody hole in them. There was a semi-revolution atmosphere around and the top brass in the Labour Movement ran away. It would have been a different political history.

I try and get a theme sometimes. It might take a fortnight to have an idea of what the theme should be at any given Gala. You've got to be topical in order to get people's attention and to actually make them feel they've heard something that's important. You have to link up the principles in which you believe with whatever is on the agenda at the time. I link things up with everyday sort of occurrences and, if it has to be 'Coronation Street', it will be. You have to talk to people on their level and that's why I embellish a lot of things that I have to say with what's happening all around us. What I

reveal about this place in here has to be said in such a way that people can understand it. So I fashion whatever I have to say in the kind of language that is best fitted to those miners who I worked with forty years ago.

Compared to the pit, the House of Commons is a doddle, no question. I've never changed, I never will. There is no comparison. When people say there are long hours, there are longer holidays as well. I refuse to accept that there's any comparison between the hard, physical nature of working underground and doing this job. I always feel extremely fortunate to be able to represent not just my own constituency but to represent the views of a lot of people on platforms like Durham. It's something I have to treasure, because I've been lucky in life. God certainly hasn't helped the Durham miners over the years.

COLLIERY

They have broken the backs
and banners of the colliery,
tipped men onto the dole
like slag into the sea.

The honest dirt ingrained in my heart,
the dirt that forms my fingerprints,
has been removed.
To make way for what?
The clean hands of tomorrow?

No.

They have broken the backs
and streets of the community,
for a few hollow victories
in the mouth of the media.

The wheel that turned the village,
dismantled and preserved.

Undermined we may be,
yet the people shall remain,
reclaiming land
in the hands and hopes
of our children.

Kevin Cadwallender

LIST OF GALA DATES AND SPEAKERS 1984 - 1994

101. 1984 —No Gala.

102. 1985, July 13th.—Tony Benn, M.P.; Jimmy Knapp; Arthur Scargill, President of National Union of Mineworkers; Neil G. Kinnock, M.P.

103. 1986, July 12th.—Dennis Skinner, M.P.; Ron Todd; Peter Heathfield, Secretary, National Union of Mineworkers; Neil Kinnock, M.P.

104. 1987, July 11th.—Tony Benn, M.P.; Rodney Bickerstaffe; Arthur Scargill, President, National Union of Mineworkers; Neil Kinnock, M.P.

105. 1988, July 16th.—Dennis Skinner, M.P.; Tony Dubbins; Peter Heathfield, Secretary, National Union of Mineworkers.

106. 1989, July 25th.—Ron Todd; Tony Benn, M.P.; Arthur Scargill, President, National Union of Mineworkers; Neil Kinnock, M.P.

107. 1990, July 14th.—Rodney Bickerstaffe; Dennis Skinner, M.P.; Arthur Scargill, President, National Union of Mineworkers.

108. 1991, July 13th.—John Prescott, M.P.; Bill Morris; Peter Heathfield, Secretary, National Union of Mineworkers.

109. 1992, July 11th.—Tony Benn, M.P.; Dennis Skinner, M.P.; Arthur Scargill, President, National Union of Mineworkers.

110. 1993, July 10th.—Tony Benn. M.P.; Dennis Skinner, M.P.; Arthur Scargill, President, National Union of Mineworkers.

111. 1994, July 9th.—Tony Benn, M.P.; Alice Mahon, M.P.; Rodney Bickerstaffe; Frank Cave, Vice President, National Union of Mineworkers.